W9-BSU-360

Ladies' Home Journal®

100 GREAT

HEALTHY

MAIN DISHES

LADIES' HOME JOURNAL™ BOOKS
New York/Des Moines

LADIES' HOME JOURNAL™ BOOKS
An Imprint of Meredith® Books

100 GREAT HEALTHY MAIN DISHES
Editor: Shelli McConnell
Writer/Researcher: Carol Prager
Copy Editor: Jennifer Miller
Associate Art Director: Tom Wegner
Electronic Production Coordinator: Paula Forest
Food Stylist: Rick Ellis
Prop Stylist: Bette Blau
Photographers: Corinne Colen Photography; Rita Maas (page 24)
Production Manager: Douglas Johnston

Vice President and Editorial Director: Elizabeth P. Rice
Executive Editor: Kay Sanders
Art Director: Ernest Shelton
Managing Editor: Christopher Cavanaugh

President, Book Group: Joseph J. Ward
Vice President, Retail Marketing: Jamie L. Martin
Vice President, Direct Marketing: Timothy Jarrell

LADIES' HOME JOURNAL®
Publishing Director and Editor-in-Chief: Myrna Blyth
Food Editor: Jan Turner Hazard
Associate Food Editors: Susan Sarao Westmoreland, Lisa Brainerd

On the cover: Jamaican Jerk Chicken with Pineapple Salsa (page 135)

Meredith Corporation
Chairman of the Executive Committee: E. T. Meredith III
Chairman of the Board, President and Chief Executive Officer: Jack D. Rehm
President and Chief Operating Officer: William T. Kerr

We Care!
All of us at Ladies' Home Journal™ Books are dedicated to providing you with the ideas and
recipe information you need to create wonderful foods. We welcome your comments and
suggestions. Write us at: Ladies' Home Journal™ Books, Cookbook Editorial Department,
RW-240, 1716 Locust St., Des Moines, IA 50309-3023.

If you would like to order additional copies of any of our books, call 1-800-678-2803.

To ensure that Ladies' Home Journal® recipes
meet the highest standards for flavor, nutrition,
appearance and reliability, we test them a
minimum of three times in our own kitchen.
That makes for quality you can count on.

Here's to Your Health

Good news! This cookbook can help put you on the road to good health. Ladies' Home Journal® has modified some of our favorite recipes to trim the fat and calories. These classic main dishes contain 500 calories or less and no more than 15 grams of fat, thus meeting healthful nutritional guidelines of 3 or less grams of fat per 100 calories. You'll find both family favorites and entertaining classics among this collection of delectable recipes. And, all those recipes are lean in every way but taste and nutrition.

CONTENTS

Healthy Family Favorites

Familiar foods made lighter—a collection for the entire family to enjoy.

Meatless Fare

Hearty, healthful recipes that are big on vegetables, grains, and legumes.

Simply Seafood

Splendid entrées featuring fresh-from-the-sea specialties.

Classics with a Light Touch
Beloved classics slimmed down. Each light bite is as luscious as the original.

Spice it Up
Some are just hot, some are simply spicy, and some are a combo of hot-and-spicy.

Index

HEALTHY FAMILY

FAVORITES

Each of these main dishes is designed
for real home cooking. Each is tailor-
made to delight the whole family.
Both quick and healthy, offerings such as
Steak and Slaw Sandwich, Mustard-
Glazed Ham Steak, and Lemon-Garlic
Chicken and Vegetables, let you skimp
on time—not nutrition or great taste.

OFF TO A GOOD START

In a healthy, balanced diet, there's no such thing as good or bad food—just good choices and common sense. What's most important is the total amount of fat and calories per day, not the fat or calorie content of a single meal. As a rule, in our healthy main dishes, there are no more than 3 grams of fat per 100 calories, with the maximum calories per meal at 500 with no more than 15 grams of fat. But flexibility is allowed. If you decide to splurge a bit at dinnertime with a special entree for friends or family, use moderation during the rest of the day.

YOUR PERSONAL CALORIE AND FAT BUDGET

To figure out the maximum daily amount of fat you should be eating, you need to know the average amount of calories you can usually consume in one day without gaining or losing weight. But you needn't keep a complicated food diary to find that out. Assuming you have a moderate activity level and your weight doesn't fluctuate, you can use this simple standard formula:

WOMEN: Body weight x 15 = calories consumed

MEN: Body weight x 17 = calories consumed

(For example, a moderately active 120-pound woman, regardless of height, consumes about 1,800 calories daily.)

Then find your calorie intake below, and check your fat allowance. We've calculated this allowance according to the American Heart Association's recommendation that no more than 30 percent of your daily calorie intake should come from fat. (Your saturated fat should not be more than 10 percent.)

Calories per day:	Fat budget:
1,200	40 grams or less
1,500	50 grams or less
1,800 to 2,000	60 grams or less
2,100	70 grams or less
2,400	80 grams or less
2,700	90 grams or less

ROAST TURKEY BREAST WITH FRUITED STUFFING

Why wait for Thanksgiving when you can serve this simple and delicious turkey dish any day of the week? Instead of hassling with a whole turkey, just roast an easy-to-handle turkey breast.

▼ *Low-fat*
▽ *Low-calorie*
  Prep time: 15 minutes
  Cooking time: 2 hours
○ *Degree of difficulty: easy*

4	**pounds turkey breast**
	Salt
	Freshly ground pepper
5	**slices whole wheat bread, cubed**
½	**cup diced celery**
⅓	**cup chopped onion**
¼	**cup pitted dates, chopped**
¼	**cup water**
2	**garlic cloves, minced**
1	**pear, cored and chopped**
⅛	**teaspoon thyme**
⅛	**teaspoon rosemary**
1	**tablespoon all-purpose flour**
½	**cup chicken broth, defatted (see tip, page 9)**

1 Preheat oven to 325°F. Season the turkey breast with salt and pepper. Place turkey breast skin side up on a rack set in a roasting pan and tent with foil. Roast 2 hours, until an oven thermometer inserted in thickest part reaches 180°F. Remove the foil during last hour.

2 Meanwhile, stir together the bread, celery, onion, dates, water, garlic, pear, thyme, and rosemary in a large bowl. Spoon the stuffing into a 1½-quart casserole. Bake 30 minutes.

3 Transfer the turkey breast to a platter. Place the roasting pan in the freezer for 10 minutes. Skim off fat. Transfer the drippings to a small saucepan and heat over low heat. Blend the flour with the chicken broth in a small bowl. Whisk into drippings and simmer 5 minutes, until thickened. Season the gravy with salt and pepper. Carve the turkey into thin slices and serve with stuffing and gravy. Makes 8 servings.

PER SERVING		DAILY GOAL
Calories	270	2,000 (F), 2,500 (M)
Total Fat	2 g	60 g or less (F), 70 g or less (M)
Saturated fat	1 g	20 g or less (F), 23 g or less (M)
Cholesterol	117 mg	300 mg or less
Sodium	246 mg	2,400 mg or less
Carbohydrates	17 g	250 g or more
Protein	45 g	55 g to 90 g

TO DEFAT BEEF OR CHICKEN BROTH

Freeze the broth for 30 minutes or refrigerate 4 hours or overnight until the fat solidifies on the surface. Remove fat from surface with a slotted spoon.

NOTES

BARBECUED TURKEY WITH FRIES AND CREAMY COLESLAW

Down-home taste makes this low-fat dinner a winner. We gave the oven-"fried" potatoes a sweet-spicy flavor. Salsa-style ketchup comes in two heat levels, so this barbeque can be hot, or not. *Also pictured on page 6.*

▼ *Low-fat*
▽ *Low-calorie*
 Prep time: 20 minutes
 Cooking time: 40 minutes
○ *Degree of difficulty: easy*

Fries
2½ pounds baking potatoes, scrubbed
1 teaspoon vegetable oil
1 tablespoon granulated sugar
1 teaspoon salt
¼ teaspoon ground red pepper

Creamy Coleslaw
⅓ cup plain nonfat yogurt
1 tablespoon fresh lemon juice
1 teaspoon honey
¼ teaspoon salt
⅛ teaspoon freshly ground pepper
3 cups thinly sliced green cabbage
1 Granny Smith apple, cored and julienned
2 green onions, julienned

Barbecued Turkey
1 teaspoon vegetable oil, divided
4 turkey breast cutlets (1 pound)
 Salt
 Freshly ground pepper
½ cup mild *or* medium salsa-style ketchup
1 tablespoon firmly packed brown sugar
4 lemon slices

1 For the Fries, preheat oven to 450°F. Line a cookie sheet with foil; coat with vegetable cooking spray. Cut the potatoes lengthwise into ½-inch sticks. Toss with oil in a large bowl to coat. Sprinkle the potatoes with sugar, salt, and red pepper and toss again. Spread potatoes in an even layer on the prepared cookie sheet. Bake 30 minutes, until golden. Immediately remove the fries from the pan.

2 Meanwhile, for the Creamy Coleslaw, combine the yogurt, lemon juice, honey, salt, and pepper in a large bowl. Add the cabbage, apple, and green onions and toss to combine.

3 For the Barbecued Turkey, heat ½ teaspoon of the oil in a large nonstick skillet over medium-high heat. Pat the turkey dry on paper towels and sprinkle lightly with salt and pepper. Add half the turkey to the skillet and cook 1 minute per side, until golden. Set aside on a plate. Repeat cooking with the remaining ½ teaspoon oil and the turkey.

4 Combine the salsa-style ketchup and brown sugar in a bowl, then stir the mixture into the skillet. Return the turkey to the skillet with the lemon slices and simmer 5 minutes. Serve with Fries and Creamy Coleslaw. Makes 4 servings.

PER SERVING		DAILY GOAL
Calories	465	2,000 (F), 2,500 (M)
Total Fat	4 g	60 g or less (F), 70 g or less (M)
Saturated fat	1 g	20 g or less (F), 23 g or less (M)
Cholesterol	71 mg	300 mg or less
Sodium	1,102 mg	2,400 mg or less
Carbohydrates	72 g	250 g or more
Protein	36 g	55 g to 90 g

CHILI CON CARNE

Here's a vat of chili that's family-friendly and not too hot or spicy. To keep things lean, we've cooked this up with ground turkey but ground chicken or beef are tasty too.

▼ *Low-fat*
▽ *Low-calorie*
  Prep time: 10 minutes
  Cooking time: 1¾ hours
○ *Degree of difficulty: easy*

  2 teaspoons vegetable oil
  1 cup chopped onions
  1 cup chopped celery
1½ teaspoons minced garlic
  1 pound ground turkey
  1 can (28 ounces) tomatoes, cut up
      with their liquid
  1 can (13¾ or 14½ ounces) beef or
      chicken broth, defatted
      (see tip, page 9)
  2 to 3 teaspoons chili powder
  1 teaspoon cumin
  ¾ teaspoon salt
  ½ teaspoon oregano

  ¼ teaspoon freshly ground pepper
  2 cans (16 ounces each) pinto, red, or
      black beans, drained and rinsed
  1 cup frozen whole-kernel corn
  1 tablespoon chopped fresh parsley

1 Heat the oil in a large Dutch oven over high heat. Add the onions, celery, and garlic and cook 3 minutes, until vegetables are softened. Add the turkey and cook, breaking up the meat with a spoon, 5 minutes, until lightly browned.

2 Add the tomatoes with liquid, beef or chicken broth, chili powder to taste, cumin, salt, oregano, and pepper; bring to a boil. Reduce heat to low. Cover and simmer 1 hour. Add the beans and corn; cover and simmer 15 minutes.

3 Increase heat to medium. Uncover the chili and cook and stir until thickened, about 15 minutes more. Stir in the parsley. Makes 10 cups.

PER CUP SERVING		DAILY GOAL
Calories	170	2,000 (F), 2,500 (M)
Total Fat	5 g	60 g or less (F), 70 g or less (M)
Saturated fat	1 g	20 g or less (F), 23 g or less (M)
Cholesterol	33 mg	300 mg or less
Sodium	687 mg	2,400 mg or less
Carbohydrates	18 g	250 g or more
Protein	13 g	55 g to 90 g

GARDEN-FRESH PIZZA

Your family's going to love this pizza. It features a nutty whole wheat crust topped with hearty tomato sauce and lots of veggies. Use low-fat cheeses and omit the turkey sausage, if desired.

▼ *Low-fat*
▽ *Low-calorie*
  Prep time: 50 minutes
  Cooking time: 42 to 45 minutes
⊖ *Degree of difficulty: moderate*

  ½ cup chopped onion
  ½ teaspoon minced garlic
  3 tablespoons water
  1 can (14½ or 16 ounces) plum
      tomatoes, with their liquid
  1 tablespoon tomato paste
  2 tablespoons chopped fresh parsley
  ¼ teaspoon oregano
  ¼ teaspoon salt
  ¼ teaspoon freshly ground pepper
      Pinch red pepper flakes
  4 ounces turkey sausage (optional)
  1 cup fresh mushrooms, sliced
      Whole Wheat Pizza Dough
      (recipe at right)

1 cup broccoli florets
1 cup sliced red onions
1 tablespoon water
¼ cup freshly grated Parmesan cheese, divided
1 cup (4 ounces) shredded part-skim mozzarella cheese
2 cups spinach leaves, julienned
1 yellow pepper, julienned

1 Combine the onion, garlic, and water in a medium saucepan. Cook over medium heat until the water is evaporated. Add the tomatoes with liquid, tomato paste, parsley, oregano, salt, pepper, and pepper flakes, breaking up the tomatoes with a spoon. Simmer 20 minutes, then set aside.

2 Remove the sausage from its casing and crumble it into a large nonstick skillet. Cook over medium-high heat 2 to 3 minutes, until browned. Drain sausage on paper towels. Pour off any drippings from the skillet; add the mushrooms and cook, stirring, 3 minutes, until all the liquid has evaporated. Remove from skillet and set aside.

3 Meanwhile, preheat oven to 425°F. Lightly oil a 12-inch pizza pan. Press the Whole Wheat Pizza Dough into the pan and prick with a fork. Bake 12 minutes, until browned.

4 Add the broccoli, onions, and water to the skillet. Cover and steam vegetables 2 minutes. Drain the vegetables on paper towels.

5 Spread the tomato sauce over the crust. Sprinkle the pizza with 2 tablespoons of the Parmesan and all of the mozzarella, then top with vegetables and sausage. Sprinkle with the remaining 2 tablespoons Parmesan. Bake 20 minutes, until vegetables are hot. Makes 4 servings.

PER SERVING		DAILY GOAL
Calories	370	2,000 (F), 2,500 (M)
Total Fat	10 g	60 g or less (F), 70 g or less (M)
Saturated fat	4 g	20 g or less (F), 23 g or less (M)
Cholesterol	21 mg	300 mg or less
Sodium	1,164 mg	2,400 mg or less
Carbohydrates	52 g	250 g or more
Protein	20 g	55 g to 90 g

WHOLE WHEAT PIZZA DOUGH

Prep time: 10 minutes plus rising
Degree of difficulty: easy

1 package rapid-rise yeast
1 teaspoon granulated sugar
½ cup warm water (105°F. to 115°F.)
¾ cup whole wheat flour
¾ cup all-purpose flour
1 teaspoon salt
1½ teaspoons olive oil

1 Dissolve the yeast and sugar in the warm water in a small bowl and let stand 2 minutes.

2 Combine the whole wheat and all-purpose flours and salt in a food processor fitted with a steel blade. Pulse twice to combine. Add yeast mixture and pulse just until moistened. With the machine on, pour the oil through the feed tube and process just until the dough begins to leave the sides of bowl and forms a ball.

3 On a lightly floured surface, knead dough until smooth and elastic, 1 minute. Shape the dough into a ball and place it in a bowl. Cover the dough and let it rise in a warm, draft-free place 25 minutes, until doubled in bulk. Makes one 12-inch crust.

SPICY OVEN-FRIED CHICKEN

We've decreased the oil but added just the right amount of heat and spice to make this crispy chicken a new family favorite.

▼ *Low-fat*
▽ *Low-calorie*
   Prep time: 15 minutes
   Cooking time: 30 minutes
○ *Degree of difficulty: easy*

Vegetable cooking spray
⅓ **cup buttermilk**
2 **teaspoons hot pepper sauce**
4 **large chicken breast halves**
   (8 ounces each)
¼ **cup seasoned dry bread crumbs**
¼ **cup yellow cornmeal**
1 **teaspoon salt**
1 **teaspoon chili powder**
1 **teaspoon dried coriander**
½ **teaspoon cumin**
¼ **teaspoon ground red pepper**

1 Preheat oven to 425°F. Coat a cookie sheet with vegetable cooking spray.

2 Combine the buttermilk and hot pepper sauce in a 13x9-inch baking dish. Remove the skin and fat from the chicken breasts and discard. Rinse chicken under cold running water and pat it dry with paper towels. Place the chicken in butter-milk mixture, turning to coat. Set aside.

3 Combine the bread crumbs, cornmeal, salt, chili powder, coriander, cumin, and ground red pepper in a shallow plate. Dip chicken in crumb mixture, turning to coat well. Place chicken, meat side up, on prepared cookie sheet. Coat chicken with vegetable cooking spray.

4 Bake 20 minutes. Remove cookie sheet from oven and coat chicken again with vegetable cooking spray. Bake 10 to 15 minutes more, until juices run clear when chicken is pierced with a knife. Makes 4 servings.

PER SERVING		DAILY GOAL
Calories	240	2,000 (F), 2,500 (M)
Total Fat	3 g	60 g or less (F), 70 g or less (M)
Saturated fat	1 g	20 g or less (F), 23 g or less (M)
Cholesterol	86 mg	300 mg or less
Sodium	939 mg	2,400 mg or less
Carbohydrates	13 g	250 g or more
Protein	37 g	55 g to 90 g

14

GRILLED CHICKEN FAJITAS

Top this south-of-the-border chicken with your favorite prepared salsa, hot or mild. We like the fresh refrigerated salsas, now available in many supermarkets.

▼ *Low-fat*
▽ *Low-calorie*
  Prep time: 20 minutes plus marinating
  Grilling time: 8 minutes
○ *Degree of difficulty: easy*

2 tablespoons fresh lime juice
1 tablespoon minced onion
1 garlic clove, minced
½ teaspoon salt
½ teaspoon oregano
⅛ teaspoon cumin
4 boneless, skinless chicken breast halves (1 pound)
4 large corn *or* flour tortillas, heated
2 cups shredded iceberg lettuce
1 tomato, diced
½ cup diced green, yellow, *or* red pepper
4 tablespoons prepared salsa

1 Combine the lime juice, onion, garlic, salt, oregano, and cumin in a shallow dish. Add the chicken, turning to coat. Cover and refrigerate 4 hours or overnight.

2 Prepare the grill or preheat the broiler and broiler pan. Grill or broil chicken 4 inches from the heat source 4 minutes per side.

3 Slice chicken across the grain into ½-inch strips. Place chicken on heated tortillas and top with lettuce, tomato, pepper, and salsa. Makes 4 servings.

PER SERVING		DAILY GOAL
Calories	205	2,000 (F), 2,500 (M)
Total Fat	2 g	60 g or less (F), 70 g or less (M)
Saturated fat	.5 g	20 g or less (F), 23 g or less (M)
Cholesterol	66 mg	300 mg or less
Sodium	483 mg	2,400 mg or less
Carbohydrates	17 g	250 g or more
Protein	28 g	55 g to 90 g

HONEY-ORANGE CHICKEN

Everyone loves chicken—especially the cook when it's this easy. Fresh sliced oranges added toward the end of the baking time gives the bird a super fresh flavor.

▼ *Low-fat*
▽ *Low-calorie*
  Prep time: 5 minutes
  Cooking time: 50 to 55 minutes
○ *Degree of difficulty: easy*

2 pounds bone-in chicken thighs *or* breasts, skin removed
½ teaspoon salt
¼ teaspoon freshly ground pepper
⅓ cup orange juice
2 tablespoons honey
2 teaspoons soy sauce
½ teaspoon ginger
2 oranges, halved and sliced
  Cooked white-and-wild rice mixture

1 Preheat oven to 375°F. Arrange the chicken in a 12x8-inch baking dish and sprinkle with salt and pepper.

2 Combine the orange juice, honey, soy sauce, and ginger in a cup until blended. Pour the sauce over the chicken. Bake 40 minutes, turning chicken twice. Arrange the sliced oranges over chicken and bake 10 to 15 minutes more. Serve with rice mixture. Makes 4 servings.

PER SERVING WITHOUT RICE		DAILY GOAL
Calories	280	2,000 (F), 2,500 (M)
Total Fat	7 g	60 g or less (F), 70 g or less (M)
Saturated fat	2 g	20 g or less (F), 23 g or less (M)
Cholesterol	138 mg	300 mg or less
Sodium	588 mg	2,400 mg or less
Carbohydrates	20 g	250 g or more
Protein	33 g	55 g to 90 g

HARVEST BEAN AND VEGETABLE SOUP

Chopped veggies and fresh lemon peel pack this satisfying, low-sodium soup with plenty of flavor. Serve this hearty soup with squares of Italian foccacia bread.

▼ *Low-fat*
▽ *Low-calorie*
    Prep time: 25 minutes
    Cooking time: 30 minutes
○ *Degree of difficulty: easy*

1   teaspoon vegetable oil
1   cup finely chopped onions
½   cup finely chopped celery
2   teaspoons minced garlic
2   cups cooked white beans (cooked without salt)
1   cup finely diced butternut squash
1   cup chopped carrots
1   can (13¾ *or* 14½ ounces) reduced-sodium chicken broth, defatted (see tip, page 9)
1   cup water
1   strip (2 inches) lemon peel
¼   teaspoon freshly ground pepper
⅛   teaspoon thyme
4   cups shredded cabbage
1   can (14½ *or* 16 ounces) whole reduced-sodium tomatoes, with their liquid
1   teaspoon fresh lemon juice
½   cup julienned fresh basil
1   teaspoon grated lemon peel

1 Heat the oil in a large saucepan over medium heat. Add the onions and celery; cover and cook, stirring occasionally, 5 minutes, until tender. Stir in the garlic and cook 30 seconds.

2 Add the beans, squash, carrots, chicken broth, water, the strip of lemon peel, pepper, and thyme; bring to a boil. Reduce heat and simmer, uncovered, 20 minutes until vegetables are tender.

3 Stir in the cabbage and cook 5 minutes, just until cabbage is tender. Stir in the tomatoes with liquid and lemon juice and return to a boil. Add the basil and grated lemon peel and serve immediately. Makes 6 servings.

PER SERVING		DAILY GOAL
Calories	155	2,000 (F), 2,500 (M)
Total Fat	1 g	60 g or less (F), 70 g or less (M)
Saturated fat	0 g	20 g or less (F), 23 g or less (M)
Cholesterol	0 mg	300 mg or less
Sodium	251 mg	2,400 mg or less
Carbohydrates	29 g	250 g or more
Protein	9 g	55 g to 90 g

NOTES

LEMON-GARLIC CHICKEN AND VEGETABLES

This versatile dish features skinless, bone-in chicken thighs, the newest cut available in the supermarket meat section. If your market doesn't have this cut, regular thighs will do—just remove the skin. You can even substitute skinless chicken breasts, but roast them for only thirty minutes.

▼ *Low-fat*
▽ *Low-calorie*
   Prep time: 15 minutes
   Cooking time: 40 minutes
○ *Degree of difficulty: easy*

3 **teaspoons vegetable oil, divided**
3 **teaspoons minced garlic, divided**
1 **teaspoon grated lemon peel**
½ **teaspoon thyme**
1½ **teaspoons salt, divided**
1 **teaspoon freshly ground pepper, divided**
6 **chicken thighs (2 pounds), skin removed**
4 **small red onions, quartered**

1 **bunch (1¼ pounds) broccoli, cut into spears**
4 **zucchini (1¾ pounds), halved, then quartered lengthwise**
2 **red peppers, cut into ½-inch strips**

1 Preheat oven to 450°F. Combine 1 teaspoon of the oil, 1 teaspoon of the garlic, the lemon peel, thyme, ½ teaspoon of the salt, and ½ teaspoon of the pepper in a large bowl. Add the chicken and onions; toss well to coat. Spread the chicken and onions on a jelly-roll pan and roast 40 minutes.

2 Combine the remaining 2 teaspoons oil, 2 teaspoons garlic, 1 teaspoon salt, and ½ teaspoon pepper in a large bowl. Add the broccoli, zucchini, and red peppers; toss well to coat. Spread vegetables on another jelly-roll pan. Halfway through the roasting time, add the vegetables to oven and continue roasting chicken and vegetables 20 minutes more. Makes 6 servings.

PER SERVING		DAILY GOAL
Calories	210	2,000 (F), 2,500 (M)
Total Fat	6 g	60 g or less (F), 70 g or less (M)
Saturated fat	1 g	20 g or less (F), 23 g or less (M)
Cholesterol	72 mg	300 mg or less
Sodium	662 mg	2,400 mg or less
Carbohydrates	18 g	250 g or more
Protein	23 g	55 g to 90 g

NOTES

SUPER SIDES

We've taken a lot of the fat out of some of your favorite side dishes. Serve these with lean broiled steak, skinless chicken breasts, or fish fillets.

OVEN-ROASTED FRIES

▼ Low-fat
▽ Low-calorie
  Prep time: 10 minutes
  Cooking time: 20 to 25 minutes
○ Degree of difficulty: easy

Preheat oven to 450°F. Line a cookie sheet with foil and brush with 1 teaspoon olive oil. Cut 4 large, scrubbed baking potatoes (2½ pounds) lengthwise into ½-inch-thick wedges. Transfer the wedges to a large bowl. Add 1 teaspoon olive oil, 1 teaspoon salt, and ¼ teaspoon freshly ground pepper and toss to coat. Spread the potatoes in a single layer on prepared cookie sheet. Bake 20 to 25 minutes, until golden and crisp. Serve immediately. Makes 4 servings.

PER SERVING		DAILY GOAL
Calories	230	2,000 (F), 2,500 (M)
Total Fat	2.5 g	60 g or less (F), 70 g or less (M)
Saturated fat	.5 g	20 g or less (F), 23 g or less (M)
Cholesterol	0 mg	300 mg or less
Sodium	705 mg	2,400 mg or less
Carbohydrates	47 g	250 g or more
Protein	6 g	55 g to 90 g

PINTO BEAN RAGOUT

▼ Low-fat
▽ Low-calorie
  Prep time: 15 minutes
  Cooking time: 15 minutes
○ Degree of difficulty: easy

Cook 1 slice of bacon in a large skillet over medium-high heat until crisp. Remove with a slotted spoon and drain on a paper towel. Pour off all but 1 tablespoon of the drippings from skillet. Add ½ cup chopped onion; 1 medium carrot, cut into ¼-inch dice; and ¼ teaspoon each salt, freshly ground pepper, and thyme.

Cook vegetables, stirring occasionally, over medium-high heat 5 minutes, until the onion is tender. Stir in 1 tablespoon tomato paste and ½ teaspoon minced garlic; and cook 1 minute. Add 1 can (14½ ounces) stewed tomatoes; 1 can (16 ounces) pinto beans, rinsed and drained; 2 tablespoons chopped fresh parsley; and 2 teaspoons red wine vinegar. Crumble the bacon and stir it into pan, then simmer 5 minutes more. Makes 2½ cups.

PER 1/2 CUP		DAILY GOAL
Calories	115	2,000 (F), 2,500 (M)
Total Fat	3 g	60 g or less (F), 70 g or less (M)
Saturated fat	1 g	20 g or less (F), 23 g or less (M)
Cholesterol	3 mg	300 mg or less
Sodium	529 mg	2,400 mg or less
Carbohydrates	17 g	250 g or more
Protein	5 g	55 g to 90 g

FENNEL MASHED POTATOES

▽ Low-calorie
  Prep time: 15 minutes
  Cooking time: 35 to 40 minutes
○ Degree of difficulty: easy

Heat 1 tablespoon butter or margarine in a large skillet over medium-high heat. Add 1 large fennel bulb (1½ pounds), cut into ½-inch pieces; ¼ cup chopped onion; ½ teaspoon salt; and ¼ teaspoon freshly ground pepper. Cook, stirring occasionally, about 10 minutes, until fennel is golden. Stir in 2 tablespoons water. Reduce heat to low; cover and simmer 10 minutes more, until the fennel is very tender. Meanwhile, bring a large saucepan of water to a boil. Add 1½ pounds all-purpose potatoes, peeled and halved (or quartered if large), and ½ teaspoon salt. Cover and cook 15 to 17 minutes, until tender. Drain potatoes in a large colander; return to saucepan. With a potato masher, mash the potatoes with 1 tablespoon butter, then add ¼ to ⅓ cup milk, 2 tablespoons chopped fresh parsley, and ½ teaspoon salt. Mash the potatoes until smooth. Stir in the fennel mixture. Makes 3½ cups.

PER 1/2 CUP		DAILY GOAL
Calories	110	2,000 (F), 2,500 (M)
Total Fat	4 g	60 g or less (F), 70 g or less (M)
Saturated fat	2 g	20 g or less (F), 23 g or less (M)
Cholesterol	10 mg	300 mg or less
Sodium	523 mg	2,400 mg or less
Carbohydrates	17 g	250 g or more
Protein	3 g	55 g to 90 g

SPINACH-FETA ORZO

▼ *Low-fat*
▽ *Low-calorie*
  Prep time: 15 minutes
  Cooking time: 20 minutes
O *Degree of difficulty: easy*

Cook 1¼ cups orzo pasta according to package directions. Meanwhile, heat 1 tablespoon olive oil in a large skillet over medium-high heat. Add ½ cup chopped onion and cook until tender. Stir in ½ teaspoon minced garlic, ½ teaspoon salt, and ¼ teaspoon freshly ground pepper; cook 1 minute. Add 1 cup chopped plum or cherry tomatoes, 1 tablespoon chopped fresh dill or 1 teaspoon dillweed, and ½ teaspoon dried mint; cook 2 minutes. Add half of 1 package (10 ounces) fresh spinach, stems removed and chopped, and cook 2 to 3 minutes, until wilted. Stir in ½ cup (2 ounces) crumbled feta cheese, 2 teaspoons fresh lemon juice, and the cooked orzo and heat through. Makes 4 cups.

PER 1/2 CUP		DAILY GOAL
Calories	160	2,000 (F), 2,500 (M)
Total Fat	4 g	60 g or less (F), 70 g or less (M)
Saturated fat	1 g	20 g or less (F), 23 g or less (M)
Cholesterol	6 mg	300 mg or less
Sodium	231 mg	2,400 mg or less
Carbohydrates	26 g	250 g or more
Protein	6 g	55 g to 90 g

SPANISH RICE

▼ *Low-fat*
▽ *Low-calorie*
  Prep time: 5 minutes
  Cooking time: 30 to 35 minutes
O *Degree of difficulty: easy*

Heat 1 tablespoon olive oil in a large skillet over medium-high heat. Add 1 green pepper, cut into ½-inch pieces; ½ cup chopped onion; and ¼ teaspoon each salt and freshly ground pepper. Cook, stirring occasionally, about 5 minutes, until the vegetables are tender-crisp. Stir in 1 cup long-grain rice and 1 teaspoon minced garlic. Cook and stir constantly about 1 minute, until rice is opaque. Add 1 can (13¾ or 14½ ounces) chicken broth, defatted; (see tip, page 9), ¼ cup dry white wine; ¼ teaspoon paprika; and a pinch of saffron powder. Bring mixture to a boil. Stir in 1 can (14½ ounces) stewed tomatoes, breaking them up with a spoon. Reduce heat to low; cover and simmer 20 to 30 minutes, until the liquid is absorbed and the rice is tender. Stir in ⅓ cup pimiento-stuffed olives. Makes 4½ cups.

PER 1/2 CUP		DAILY GOAL
Calories	185	2,000 (F), 2,500 (M)
Total Fat	4 g	60 g or less (F), 70 g or less (M)
Saturated fat	0 g	20 g or less (F), 23 g or less (M)
Cholesterol	0 mg	300 mg or less
Sodium	788 mg	2,400 mg or less
Carbohydrates	32 g	250 g or more
Protein	4 g	55 g to 90 g

SPINACH-RICOTTA POTATOES

Most vegetables have very small amounts of fat, and potatoes are no exception. Baked potato toppings don't have to add to the fat count. We combined spinach with low-fat milk and ricotta cheese for a creamy alternative to butter. While the potatoes are in the microwave, cook up boneless, skinless chicken breasts or fish fillets to round out the meal.

Ⓜ️ *Microwave*
▼ *Low-fat*
▽ *Low-calorie*
   Prep time: 25 minutes
   Microwave time: 15 minutes
○ *Degree of difficulty: easy*

4 **medium baking potatoes**
1 **package (10 ounces) frozen chopped spinach, thawed and squeezed dry**
1 **cup part-skim ricotta cheese**
⅓ **cup low-fat (1%) milk**
½ **teaspoon salt**

¼ **teaspoon freshly ground pepper**
⅛ **teaspoon nutmeg**
1 **tablespoon freshly grated Parmesan cheese**

1 Prick the potatoes with a fork. Arrange them in a microwave oven 1 inch apart on paper towels. Microwave on high (100% power) 13 minutes, turning halfway through. Remove from oven. Wrap each potato in foil and let stand 10 minutes.

2 Meanwhile, combine the spinach, ricotta, milk, salt, pepper, and nutmeg in a medium bowl; stir until smooth. Slit each potato down the center, sprinkle lightly with salt and pepper, and fill with ½ cup spinach mixture.

3 Arrange potatoes in a 10-inch glass pie plate. Sprinkle the tops with Parmesan. Cover with wax paper, turning back one section to vent. Microwave on high (100% power) 2 minutes, until hot. Makes 4 servings.

PER SERVING		DAILY GOAL
Calories	235	2,000 (F), 2,500 (M)
Total Fat	5 g	60 g or less (F), 70 g or less (M)
Saturated fat	3 g	20 g or less (F), 23 g or less (M)
Cholesterol	19 mg	300 mg or less
Sodium	444 mg	2,400 mg or less
Carbohydrates	36 g	250 g or more
Protein	12 g	55 g to 90 g

GRILLED APRICOT-CHICKEN AND VEGETABLE SALAD

We added apricot preserves to this zesty, oil-free dressing to round out the flavor, but it's just as delicious made with orange marmalade. Grilling the sliced chicken and veggies gives them such a rich taste you'll never miss the oil.

▼ *Low-fat*
▽ *Low-calorie*
   Prep time: 20 minutes
   Grilling time: 11 to 14 minutes
○ *Degree of difficulty: easy*

1 **large baby eggplant**
1 **large red onion**
1 **large red pepper**
1 **large yellow pepper**
1 **medium zucchini**
⅓ **cup apricot preserves**
⅓ **cup balsamic vinegar**
½ **teaspoon minced garlic**
¼ **teaspoon dried rosemary, crushed**
½ **teaspoon salt, divided**

2 **boneless, skinless chicken breasts (12 ounces)**

4 **cups assorted salad greens (Boston lettuce, watercress, and arugula)**

1 Prepare grill. Quarter the eggplant lengthwise. Slice the red onion crosswise ½ inch thick. Slice the peppers lengthwise into 1½-inch-wide strips. Slice the zucchini diagonally ½ inch thick. Place the vegetables in a 13x9-inch baking dish.

2 Combine the apricot preserves, vinegar, garlic, rosemary, and ¼ teaspoon of the salt in a small saucepan. Heat to boiling, stirring frequently, over medium heat. Remove 1 tablespoon of dressing to a cup, then pour the remaining dressing over vegetables, tossing to coat.

3 Grill vegetables, in batches if necessary, over medium-hot coals, 8 to 10 minutes, until tender, turning occasionally and brushing with dressing in baking dish. Return vegetables to baking dish and toss with any remaining dressing. Set aside.

4 Sprinkle both sides of the chicken with the remaining ¼ teaspoon salt. Grill 3 to 4 minutes per side, brushing occasionally with the reserved 1 tablespoon of dressing,

until cooked through. Transfer the chicken to a cutting board and slice thin.

5 To serve, arrange the greens on a platter and top them with chicken and grilled vegetables. Makes 4 servings.

PER SERVING		DAILY GOAL
Calories	220	2,000 (F), 2,500 (M)
Total Fat	1 g	60 g or less (F), 70 g or less (M)
Saturated fat	0 g	20 g or less (F), 23 g or less (M)
Cholesterol	49 mg	300 mg or less
Sodium	357 mg	2,400 mg or less
Carbohydrates	31 g	250 g or more
Protein	23 g	55 g to 90 g

COOKING SMART 'N' HEALTHY

Reading food labels: This is probably the best place to get started. More and more packaged foods list the number of fat grams they contain. Here's some other user-friendly label lingo to know:

• Sodium-free or salt-free means a product contains no more than 5 milligrams of sodium per serving; very low sodium, no more than 35 milligrams sodium per serving; and low sodium, 140 milligrams or less per serving.

• For meat and poultry, low-fat or lean means fat content is 10 percent or less. Extra-lean meat contains 5 percent or less fat. The actual amount must be noted on the label.

• For dairy products, low-fat means ½ to 2 percent milkfat and nonfat or skim means less than ½ percent milkfat.

The Light Stuff: When a product says light or lite, always check whether the light food is low-calorie and low-fat by reading the label for the calorie and fat count per serving.

Cooking tricks of the trade:

• Use cooking methods that add little or no fat, such as baking, roasting, broiling, grilling, and stir-frying.

• Use nonstick skillets for sautéeing. When a recipe calls for greasing a pan or a cookie sheet, coat with vegetable cooking spray instead of butter or margarine.

MUSTARD-GLAZED HAM STEAK

Ⓜ   *Microwave*
▼   *Low-fat*
▽   *Low-calorie*
    Prep time: 10 minutes
    Microwave time: 12 minutes
Ｏ   *Degree of difficulty: easy*

1   **teaspoon olive oil**
¼   **cup finely chopped onion**
½   **teaspoon caraway seeds**
6   **cups thinly sliced cabbage**
1   **tablespoon Dijon mustard**
2   **teaspoons honey**
1   **teaspoon red wine vinegar**
1   **fully cooked reduced-fat ham steak
    (1 to 1¼ pounds)**
    Freshly ground pepper
1   **tablespoon chopped fresh parsley**

1   Combine the oil, onion, and caraway seeds in a shallow 2-quart microwave-proof casserole. Cover and microwave on high (100% power) 2 minutes, stirring once. Stir in the cabbage; cover and microwave on high (100% power) 3 minutes more.

2   Combine the mustard, honey, and vinegar in a cup. Place the ham steak over the cabbage and spread with mustard mixture. Cover and microwave on medium-high (70% power) 7 minutes or until ham is heated through. Sprinkle with the pepper and parsley. Makes 4 servings.

PER SERVING		DAILY GOAL
Calories	205	2,000 (F), 2,500 (M)
Total Fat	6 g	60 g or less (F), 70 g or less (M)
Saturated fat	2 g	20 g or less (F), 23 g or less (M)
Cholesterol	55 mg	300 mg or less
Sodium	1,673 mg	2,400 mg or less
Carbohydrates	10 g	250 g or more
Protein	25 g	55 g to 90 g

SPAGHETTI WITH ZUCCHINI AND LEMON

▼   *Low-fat*
    Prep time: 20 minutes
    Cooking time: 12 minutes
Ｏ   *Degree of difficulty: easy*

2   **teaspoons olive oil**
3   **ounces Canadian bacon, julienned
    (½ cup)**
1½ **pounds zucchini, thinly sliced**
½   **teaspoon salt**

½   **teaspoon freshly ground pepper**
2   **teaspoons minced garlic**
¼   **teaspoon grated lemon peel**
1   **pound spaghetti, cooked according
    to package directions and
    drained, ¼ cup hot cooking
    water reserved**
1   **tablespoon fresh lemon juice**
½   **cup julienned fresh basil**

1   Heat the oil in a large skillet over high heat. Add the Canadian bacon and cook, stirring, 2 minutes. Add the zucchini, salt, and pepper. Cook and stir 5 minutes, just until tender-crisp. Stir in the garlic and cook 1 minute.

2   Toss the vegetables with the lemon peel, hot spaghetti, reserved water, lemon juice, and basil in a large serving bowl. Makes 4 servings.

PER SERVING		DAILY GOAL
Calories	510	2,000 (F), 2,500 (M)
Total fat	6 g	60 g or less (F), 70 g or less (M)
Saturated fat	1 g	20 g or less (F), 23 g or less (M)
Cholesterol	11 mg	300 mg or less
Sodium	587 mg	2,400 mg or less
Carbohydrates	92 g	250 g or more
Protein	21 g	55 g to 90 g

CANTON PORK WITH BROCCOLI AND PEPPERS

Here's a stir-fry the whole family will love. The dish can also be prepared with boneless, skinless chicken or turkey breast. Serve the stir-fry with plenty of fluffy rice.

▽ *Low-calorie*
Prep time: 15 minutes
Cooking time: 14 to 17 minutes
○ *Degree of difficulty: easy*

¾ **cup chicken broth, defatted (see tip, page 9)**
¼ **cup reduced-sodium soy sauce**
2 **tablespoons dry sherry**
⅛ **to ¼ teaspoon red pepper flakes**
8 **ounces lean pork loin, cut into thin strips**
1 **tablespoon cornstarch**
2 **teaspoons vegetable oil, divided**
3 **dime-size slices fresh ginger, divided**
3 **cups broccoli florets**
1 **cup green beans, cut in half**
2 **tablespoons water**

8 **ounces firm tofu, cut into strips**
1 **teaspoon minced garlic**
1 **cup red pepper strips**
½ **cup sliced green onions**

1 Combine the chicken broth, soy sauce, sherry, and red pepper flakes in a medium bowl. Set aside.

2 Dust the pork with cornstarch. Heat 1 teaspoon oil over high heat in a wok or large skillet until very hot. Add one slice of the ginger, broccoli, and green beans and cook, stirring constantly, 2 minutes. Add the water and cook 2 minutes more. Remove the vegetables to a large plate and return the skillet to the heat.

3 Toss the pork with the broth mixture, then transfer it with a slotted spoon to the hot skillet. Add another slice of ginger and cook, stirring, 5 minutes. Add pork to broccoli mixture.

4 Heat the remaining 1 teaspoon oil in skillet. Add the remaining slice of ginger, tofu, garlic, red pepper strips, and green onions. Cook, stirring, 2 to 4 minutes, until pepper is just tender. Return pork and vegetables to skillet, along with remaining marinade. Cook, stirring, 3 minutes more until heated through. Makes 4 servings.

PER SERVING		DAILY GOAL
Calories	230	2,000 (F), 2,500 (M)
Total Fat	8 g	60 g or less (F), 70 g or less (M)
Saturated fat	1 g	20 g or less (F), 23 g or less (M)
Cholesterol	36 mg	300 mg or less
Sodium	887 mg	2,400 mg or less
Carbohydrates	16 g	250 g or more
Protein	23 g	55 g to 90 g

PORK CHOPS IN PLUM SAUCE

This unusual pairing of lean pork chops and plums makes an easy, elegant entrée that can be served with steamed green beans and quick-cooking brown rice.

▼ *Low-fat*
▽ *Low-calorie*
Prep time: 10 minutes
Cooking time: 15 to 18 minutes
○ *Degree of difficulty: easy*

1 **teaspoon olive oil**
4 **loin pork chops, trimmed**
½ **teaspoon salt**
¼ **teaspoon freshly ground pepper**
½ **cup finely chopped onion**

4 large plums, thinly sliced
¼ teaspoon tarragon
2 tablespoons white vinegar
½ cup chicken broth, defatted
   (see tip, page 9)
1 tablespoon firmly packed brown
   sugar

1 Heat the oil in a large nonstick skillet over medium-high heat. Sprinkle both sides of the pork with the salt and pepper. Cook 3 to 4 minutes per side until cooked through. Transfer pork to a warm platter.

2 Add the onion, plums, and tarragon to skillet and cook 2 to 3 minutes. Add the vinegar, then the broth and brown sugar. Bring the sauce to a boil and boil 3 minutes, until reduced by half. Pour sauce over chops. Makes 4 servings.

PER SERVING		DAILY GOAL
Calories	260	2,000 (F), 2,500 (M)
Total Fat	8 g	60 g or less (F), 70 g or less (M)
Saturated fat	3 g	20 g or less (F), 23 g or less (M)
Cholesterol	70 mg	300 mg or less
Sodium	483 mg	2,400 mg or less
Carbohydrates	12 g	250 g or more
Protein	26 g	55 g to 90 g

SPICY BLACK BEAN, CHORIZO, AND CORN CHOWDER

Here's soup satisfaction in minutes! Spicy chorizo sausage packs a flavor punch without adding too much fat or calories to chunky bean and vegetable chowder.

▼ *Low-fat*
▽ *Low-calorie*
   Prep time: 5 minutes
   Cooking time: 6 minutes
○ *Degree of difficulty: easy*

1 teaspoon vegetable oil
4 ounces sliced chorizo sausage *or*
   diced baked ham
1 medium onion, chopped
1 clove garlic, chopped
1 teaspoon cumin
¼ teaspoon oregano
1 can (13¾ *or* 14½ ounces) chicken
   broth, defatted (see tip, page 9)
1 can (17 ounces) corn, drained and
   rinsed

2 cans (15 *or* 15½ ounces each)
   black beans, drained and rinsed,
   divided
½ cup water
¼ cup chopped fresh cilantro
¼ teaspoon freshly ground pepper

1 Heat the oil in a large saucepan over high heat. Add the chorizo and brown, stirring, 2 minutes. Stir in the onion and garlic and cook 1 minute. Stir in the cumin and oregano and cook 30 seconds, until fragrant. Add the chicken broth, corn, and ½ cup of the beans to the saucepan.

2 Purée the remaining beans with the water in a blender until smooth; stir into the soup. Cover and bring to a boil. Reduce heat and simmer, covered, 2 minutes. Stir in the cilantro and pepper. Makes 4 servings.

PER SERVING		DAILY GOAL
Calories	300	2,000 (F), 2,500 (M)
Total Fat	7 g	60 g or less (F), 70 g or less (M)
Saturated fat	1 g	20 g or less (F), 23 g or less (M)
Cholesterol	16 mg	300 mg or less
Sodium	1,615 mg	2,400 mg or less
Carbohydrates	46 g	250 g or more
Protein	18 g	55 g to 90 g

ROAST PORK TENDERLOIN WITH BRAISED CABBAGE

Healthy cooks love pork tenderloin—the lean and tender meat right next to the loin. Although higher in price per pound than loin roast, tenderloin is a good value because there is no waste.

▼ *Low-fat*
▽ *Low-calorie*
  Prep time: 55 minutes
  Cooking time: 25 minutes
○ *Degree of difficulty: easy*

- 2 **pork tenderloins (1½ pounds total), trimmed**
- 2 **teaspoons minced garlic**
- 1¼ **teaspoons salt, divided**
- ¾ **teaspoon freshly ground pepper, divided**
- ¾ **teaspoon thyme, divided**
- 1 **cup minced onions**
- 1 **small head (2 pounds) green cabbage, cored and thinly sliced**
- 1 **Golden Delicious apple, peeled, cored, and thinly sliced**
- ¾ **cup chicken broth, defatted (see tip, page 9)**
- 1 **cup apple cider**

1 Preheat oven to 450°F. Mash the garlic with 1 teaspoon of the salt, ½ teaspoon of the pepper, and ½ teaspoon of the thyme. Rub the mixture all over the pork. Place the onions in the bottom of a small roasting pan and place pork on top. Roast 25 minutes, until juices run clear when the pork is pierced with a fork.

2 Meanwhile, combine the cabbage, apple, broth, the remaining ¼ teaspoon of salt, pepper, and thyme in a large skillet. Cover and cook over medium-high heat 10 minutes, until cabbage is tender-crisp. Cook, uncovered, 3 to 4 minutes, until most of the liquid is evaporated. Cover and keep warm.

3 Transfer pork to a serving platter; cover and keep warm. Pour the apple cider in the roasting pan and bring to a boil over high heat, stirring to scrape up onions and browned bits. Serve pork with cabbage and pan juices. Makes 6 servings.

PER SERVING		DAILY GOAL
Calories	205	2,000 (F), 2,500 (M)
Total Fat	3 g	60 g or less (F), 70 g or less (M)
Saturated fat	1 g	20 g or less (F), 23 g or less (M)
Cholesterol	74 mg	300 mg or less
Sodium	682 mg	2,400 mg or less
Carbohydrates	18 g	250 g or more
Protein	26 g	55 g to 90 g

NOTES

STEAK AND SLAW SANDWICH

When cooking this spicy steak, be sure to heat the pan until it's smoking hot (we find a cast-iron skillet works best). That way you won't need to oil the pan and the meat won't stick.

▼ *Low-fat*
▽ *Low-calorie*
  Prep time: 15 minutes
  Cooking time: 12 minutes
○ *Degree of difficulty: easy*

Slaw

1 tablespoon rice wine vinegar
2 teaspoons Dijon mustard
1 teaspoon sugar
1 teaspoon vegetable oil
½ teaspoon minced jalapeño chile
¼ teaspoon salt
⅛ teaspoon freshly ground pepper
2 cups finely shredded red cabbage
2 green onions, sliced thin

Dry Rub

½ teaspoon salt
½ teaspoon paprika
¼ teaspoon cumin
¼ teaspoon dry mustard
⅛ teaspoon freshly ground black pepper
⅛ teaspoon ground red pepper
  Pinch thyme

12 ounces beef top *or* bottom round steak, 1 inch thick (London broil), trimmed
8 thick slices crusty Italian bread, toasted

1 For Slaw, combine the vinegar, mustard, sugar, oil, jalapeño, salt, and pepper. Add the cabbage and green onions and toss well to coat. Set aside.

2 For Dry Rub, combine the salt, paprika, cumin, dry mustard, black pepper, red pepper, and thyme in a cup.

3 Heat a large cast-iron skillet over medium-high heat until almost smoking, about 5 minutes. Sprinkle the beef with the Dry Rub. Add to skillet and cook 6 minutes per side for medium-rare. Let stand 5 minutes. Slice beef very thinly and divide it evenly among 4 toast slices. Top with the Slaw and remaining toast. Makes 4 servings.

PER SERVING		DAILY GOAL	
Calories	295	2,000 (F), 2,500 (M)	
Total Fat	5 g	60 g or less (F), 70 g or less (M)	
Saturated fat	1 g	20 g or less (F), 23 g or less (M)	
Cholesterol	49 mg	300 mg or less	
Sodium	592 mg	2,400 mg or less	
Carbohydrates	36 g	250 g or more	
Protein	25 g	55 g to 90 g	

NOTES

HEARTY POT ROAST

Lean meat and lots of vegetables add up to a perfect winter meal. And what could be simpler? Everything roasts together slowly in the oven. When dinner is ready, serve it with a tossed salad.

▼ *Low-fat*
▽ *Low-calorie*
  Prep time: 20 minutes
  Cooking time: 2¾ hours
○ *Degree of difficulty: easy*

2	**pounds trimmed bottom round roast**
1½	**cups coarsely chopped onions**
2	**teaspoons ginger**
2	**teaspoons minced garlic**
1	**teaspoon ground coriander**
¼	**teaspoon cinnamon**
1½	**cups dry white wine**
1	**can (13¾ *or* 14½ ounces) beef broth, defatted (see tip, page 9), plus enough water to equal 2 cups**
1	**tablespoon molasses**
2	**3-inch strips orange peel**
½	**bay leaf**
½	**teaspoon freshly ground pepper**
3	**pounds red new potatoes, quartered**
2	**pounds carrots, cut into 2-inch pieces**
½	**teaspoon salt**
2	**tablespoons chopped fresh parsley**

1 Preheat oven to 325°F. Heat a large Dutch oven over medium-high heat until very hot. Add the beef and cook until well browned on all sides; transfer to a plate and set aside.

2 Add the onions to Dutch oven and cook until soft and beginning to brown, 10 to 15 minutes. Stir in the ginger, garlic, coriander, and cinnamon and cook 1 minute. Stir in the wine, broth, water, molasses, orange peel, bay leaf, and pepper. Return beef to the pot and bring to a boil. Cover and transfer the pot to the oven. Roast 1½ hours. (Can be made ahead. Cool. Cover and refrigerate overnight. Skim fat. Reheat to boiling over medium heat.)

3 Add the potatoes and carrots to the Dutch oven and sprinkle with the salt. Cover and roast 1 hour more. Discard bay leaf. Remove beef and slice very thinly. Serve the meat with vegetables and juices. Sprinkle with parsley. Makes 8 servings.

PER SERVING		DAILY GOAL
Calories	380	2,000 (F), 2,500 (M)
Total Fat	7 g	60 g or less (F), 70 g or less (M)
Saturated fat	2 g	20 g or less (F), 23 g or less (M)
Cholesterol	67 mg	300 mg or less
Sodium	495 mg	2,400 mg or less
Carbohydrates	48 g	250 g or more
Protein	30 g	55 g to 90 g

NOTES

31

TARRAGON-MUSTARD FLANK STEAK WITH PEPPER

This steak and veggie combo makes a super open-faced sandwich on toasted crusty bread. Serve it with our crisp Oven Fries (recipe page 11).

▼ *Low-fat*
▽ *Low-calorie*
   Prep time: 15 minutes plus standing
   Cooking time: 19 minutes
O *Degree of difficulty: easy*

1 **onion, sliced crosswise ½ inch thick**
1 **green pepper, sliced**
1 **red pepper, sliced**
1 **yellow pepper, sliced**
1 **teaspoon vegetable oil**
¼ **teaspoon salt**
   Freshly ground pepper
2 **tablespoons Dijon mustard**
½ **teaspoon minced garlic**
½ **teaspoon tarragon**
1¼ **pounds beef flank steak, fat trimmed**

1 Preheat broiler and line a broiler pan with foil.

2 Combine the onion, green, red, and yellow peppers, oil, salt, and ⅛ teaspoon pepper in a large bowl. Spread the vegetable mixture on prepared pan and broil 4 inches from heat 10 minutes, turning once. Transfer vegetables to a bowl; cover and keep warm.

3 Combine the mustard, garlic, tarragon, and ¼ teaspoon pepper in a small bowl. Spread half the mixture on one side of the meat. Broil, mustard side up, 6 minutes. Turn meat over and spread with the remaining mixture and broil 3 minutes more. Transfer the meat to a carving board and let stand 5 minutes. Cut the steak in thin, diagonal slices across the grain. Serve with vegetables. Makes 4 servings.

PER SERVING		DAILY GOAL
Calories	210	2,000 (F), 2,500 (M)
Total Fat	9 g	60 g or less (F), 70 g or less (M)
Saturated fat	3 g	20 g or less (F), 23 g or less (M)
Cholesterol	52 mg	300 mg or less
Sodium	427 mg	2,400 mg or less
Carbohydrates	52 g	250 g or more
Protein	22 g	55 g to 90 g

NOTES

BEEF AND NOODLE SOUP

It's hard to believe that such a hearty, flavorful soup could be so quick, easy, and healthful. You can even afford to stir a dollop of low-fat sour cream into each bowl at serving time.

▼   *Low-fat*
▽   *Low-calorie*
    Prep time: 10 minutes
    Cooking time: 32 minutes
O   *Degree of difficulty: easy*

1   **pound extra-lean (95%) ground beef**
1   **tablespoon vegetable oil**
1   **cup diced carrots**
1   **cup diced onions**
1   **cup sliced celery**
½   **teaspoon minced garlic**
2   **cans (13¾ *or* 14½ ounces each) chicken broth, defatted (see tip, page 9)**
1   **can (14½ *or* 16 ounces) whole tomatoes, with their liquid**
½   **teaspoon thyme**
½   **teaspoon salt**
¼   **teaspoon freshly ground pepper**
3   **cups (4 ounces) wide egg noodles, cooked according to package directions**
¼   **cup chopped fresh parsley**
    Low-fat sour cream, for garnish

1   Cook the ground beef in a large Dutch oven over medium-high heat 5 to 7 minutes, until browned. Remove meat from pan with a slotted spoon and set aside.

2   Add the oil, carrots, onions, celery, and garlic to pan and cook 5 minutes, until tender-crisp. Add the chicken broth, tomatoes with their liquid, thyme, salt, pepper, and beef, breaking up the tomatoes with a spoon; bring to a boil. Reduce heat, cover, and simmer 20 minutes.

3   Just before serving, stir the noodles and parsley into soup and heat through. Spoon into bowls and garnish each with a dollop of sour cream, if desired. Makes 8 cups.

PER CUP SERVING
WITHOUT SOUR CREAM

		DAILY GOAL
Calories	175	2,000 (F), 2,500 (M)
Total Fat	5 g	60 g or less (F), 70 g or less (M)
Saturated fat	1 g	20 g or less (F), 23 g or less (M)
Cholesterol	41 mg	300 mg or less
Sodium	877 mg	2,400 mg or less
Carbohydrates	18 g	250 g or more
Protein	14 g	55 g to 90 g

HEARTY BEEF AND VEGETABLE STEW

No browning is necessary for this rich stew. The meat and onions are first roasted without adding liquid, then the other vegetables are added and cooked until tender. Be sure to use your heaviest pot with a tight-fitting lid to keep all the moisture in.

▼ *Low-fat*
▽ *Low-calorie*
   Prep time: 50 minutes
   Cooking time: 2½ to 3 hours
○ *Degree of difficulty: easy*

2 **teaspoons minced garlic**
1½ **teaspoons salt**
2 **pounds beef round steak, trimmed of all fat, cut into 1-inch cubes**
3 **cups finely chopped onions**
½ **teaspoon thyme**
½ **teaspoon freshly ground pepper**
1 **can (14½ *or* 16 ounces) whole tomatoes, with their liquid**
2 **tablespoons tomato paste**
2 **pounds small red potatoes, halved or quartered**
2 **pounds carrots, cut into 1½-inch pieces**
1 **pound fresh mushrooms, trimmed and quartered**
1 **package (10 ounces) frozen peas, thawed**

1 Preheat oven to 325°F. With the flat side of a knife, crush the garlic with the salt to make a paste.

2 Combine the garlic paste, beef, onions, thyme, and pepper in a heavy Dutch oven. Cover and roast 1½ hours. Stir in the tomatoes with their liquid, tomato paste, potatoes, carrots, and mushrooms. Cook 1 to 1½ hours more, until the meat and vegetables are tender. Remove the stew from oven and stir in peas. Makes 10 servings.

PER SERVING		DAILY GOAL
Calories	300	2,000 (F), 2,500 (M)
Total Fat	5 g	60 g or less (F), 70 g or less (M)
Saturated fat	2 g	20 g or less (F), 23 g or less (M)
Cholesterol	53 mg	300 mg or less
Sodium	554 mg	2,400 mg or less
Carbohydrates	38 g	250 g or more
Protein	26 g	55 g to 90 g

TEX-MEX MEATLOAF

Chili powder, cumin, and corn help turn everyday meatloaf into an entrée your family will look forward to. And any leftovers make terrific sandwiches.

▼   *Low-fat*
▽   *Low-calorie*
    Prep time: 20 minutes plus cooling
    Cooking time: 75 to 80 minutes
○   *Degree of difficulty: easy*

1   teaspoon vegetable oil
1   cup finely chopped onions
1   red pepper, diced
1   tablespoon chili powder
1   teaspoon cumin
¼   teaspoon ground red pepper
1   teaspoon minced garlic
1½ pounds extra-lean (95%) ground
     beef, turkey, *or* chicken
2   cups fresh bread crumbs
1   cup canned *or* frozen whole-kernel
     corn
⅓   cup plus 2 tablespoons ketchup,
     divided
⅓   cup low-fat (1%) milk
1   large egg plus 1 large egg white
1   teaspoon salt
½   teaspoon freshly ground pepper

1   Preheat oven to 350°F. Heat the oil in a medium nonstick skillet over medium heat. Add the onions and red pepper. Cook, stirring occasionally, 5 to 10 minutes, until tender. Stir in the chili powder, cumin, ground red pepper, and garlic and cook 30 seconds more. Transfer the mixture to a large bowl and cool.

2   Add the beef to the vegetable mixture with the bread crumbs, corn, ⅓ cup of the ketchup, milk, egg, egg white, salt, and pepper and mix well. Pat the meat mixture into a 9x5-inch loaf pan. Spread the remaining 2 tablespoons ketchup on top. Bake 75 to 80 minutes. Let stand 10 minutes before slicing. Discard any drippings. Makes 8 servings.

PER SERVING		DAILY GOAL	
Calories	200	2,000 (F), 2,500 (M)	
Total Fat	5 g	60 g or less (F), 70 g or less (M)	
Saturated fat	1 g	20 g or less (F), 23 g or less (M)	
Cholesterol	69 mg	300 mg or less	
Sodium	707 mg	2,400 mg or less	
Carbohydrates	19 g	250 g or more	
Protein	20 g	55 g to 90 g	

35

MEATLESS

FARE

Served by health-conscious cooks, meals without meat are appearing on dinner tables everywhere. Brimming with vegetables, grains, and legumes, these stick-to-your ribs dishes are guaranteed to satisfy. Here, you'll find pasta favorites, from classic Macaroni-and-Cheese Cake to Whole Wheat Linguine with Spring Vegetables. Get creative with Curried Vegetable Strudel, or tri-colored Triple Potato Chowder. There's a host of tastes and textures from which to choose. We promise you won't miss the meat!

PENNE WITH FENNEL AND PEPPERS

Look for bulbs of fresh fennel with the stems and "fronds" attached. The fronds should be bright green and look like fresh dill. When chopped and added to the colorful sliced vegetables, the fronds give an extra touch of sweetness.

▼ *Low-fat*
▽ *Low-calorie*
   Prep time: 15 minutes
   Cooking time: 18 minutes
○ *Degree of difficulty: easy*

  1 **teaspoon olive oil**
  ½ **cup sliced onion**
  1 **small bulb fennel (anise) (about 8 ounces)**
  1 **medium red pepper, cut into strips**
  1 **medium yellow pepper, cut into strips**
  1 **teaspoon minced garlic**
  1 **cup chicken broth, defatted (see tip, page 9) *or* vegetable broth**
  ½ **teaspoon salt**
  ¼ **teaspoon freshly ground pepper**
  1 **pound penne *or* ziti, cooked according to package directions, drained**

1 Heat the oil in a large skillet over medium-high heat. Add the onion and cook, stirring occasionally, 4 to 5 minutes, until tender.

2 Meanwhile, cut the fronds from the fennel and chop enough fronds to equal ¼ cup; set aside. Slice fennel into thin strips. Add the fennel and peppers to skillet and cook 8 minutes, until just tender. Add the garlic and cook 30 seconds, until fragrant. Add the broth, salt, and pepper and bring to a boil. Reduce heat and simmer 5 minutes.

3 Toss the sauce with the hot pasta in a large serving bowl. Sprinkle with chopped fronds. Makes 4 servings.

PER SERVING		DAILY GOAL
Calories	465	2,000 (F), 2,500 (M)
Total fat	4 g	60 g or less (F), 70 g or less (M)
Saturated fat	1 g	20 g or less (F), 23 g or less (M)
Cholesterol	0 mg	300 mg or less
Sodium	611 mg	2,400 mg or less
Carbohydrates	90 g	250 g or more
Protein	16 g	55 g to 90 g

NOTES

THE HEALTHY PANTRY

Eating a variety of foods is the best way to get all the nutrients you need, but there are some foods that can provide an extra boost of nutrients to your family's diet. Here's a list of wonder foods for the healthy kitchen. They are low-fat, low-calorie, and packed with vitamins and minerals. Those marked with an asterisk are good sources of calcium and iron, making them especially valuable to women, who need 1,000 milligrams of calcium and 18 milligrams of iron per day to help guard against osteoporosis and anemia.

Cereals: (whole grain *iron-fortified) High in fiber and complex carbohydrates; fortified cereals are also high in many vitamins and minerals.
Oats: High fiber, fat-free
Whole-Grain Rice: High in fiber and complex carbohydrates, fat-free

Wheat Bran: High fiber
Broccoli: High in fiber and vitamin C, fat-free
Carrots: High in fiber and vitamin A, fat-free
Cauliflower: High fiber, good source of vitamin C, fat-free
Corn: High in fiber and complex carbohydrates, fair source of potassium
*****Kale:** High in vitamin A, fair source of calcium, fat-free
Potatoes: High in fiber, vitamin C, and potassium, fat-free
*****Spinach:** High in vitamin A, fat-free
Squash: High in fiber, vitamins C and A (some varieties), fat-free
Tomatoes: High in fiber and vitamin A, good source of vitamin C, fat-free
Bananas: High in potassium and fiber, virtually fat-free
Blueberries: High fiber, fat-free
Cantaloupe: High in fiber, vitamins C and A, fat-free

Oranges: High in fiber and vitamin C, good source of potassium, fat-free
Strawberries: High in fiber and vitamin C, fat-free
*****Cheese** (especially lower fat varieties): High protein, good source of calcium
*****Low-fat Cottage Cheese:** High protein, good source of calcium
*****Low-fat or skim milk:** High in protein and calcium
*****Nonfat Dry Milk:** Good source of protein and calcium
*****Nonfat or Low-fat Yogurt** (regular or frozen): High in calcium and protein
*****Legumes** (such as black beans, black-eye peas, chick-peas, kidney beans, lentils, lima beans, split peas, pinto beans, navy and white beans, soybeans): High in potassium and fiber, good source of complex carbohydrates and protein
*****Tofu** (processed with calcium sulfate): High in calcium

WHOLE WHEAT LINGUINE WITH SPRING VEGETABLES

This gorgeous pasta dish is adapted from Seppi Renggli, former chef of New York City's famed Four Seasons Restaurant, and a pioneer in the creation of spa cuisine. *Also pictured on page 36.*

▼ *Low-fat*
▽ *Low-calorie*
   Prep time: 20 minutes
   Cooking time: 8 to 10 minutes
○ *Degree of difficulty: easy*

2 teaspoons olive oil
2 large shallots, thinly sliced
1 teaspoon minced garlic
1 jalapeño chile, seeded and minced
¾ cup thinly sliced celery
¾ cup thinly sliced carrot
1 cup small broccoli florets
8 ounces asparagus, thinly sliced on the diagonal
1 small zucchini, thinly sliced on the diagonal
2 cups sliced fresh shiitake *or* white mushrooms
4 ounces snow peas, trimmed and halved diagonally
¾ cup chicken broth, defatted (see tip, page 9), *or* vegetable broth
6 ounces whole wheat linguine, cooked according to package directions, drained
½ teaspoon salt
¼ teaspoon freshly ground pepper
2 tablespoons chopped chives

1 Heat the oil in a large skillet over high heat. Add the shallots, garlic, and jalapeño and cook 1 minute, until soft. Add the celery and carrots and cook 1 minute. Stir in the broccoli, asparagus, zucchini, mushrooms, snow peas, and chicken broth. Cover and cook 3 minutes.

2 Add the hot linguine, salt, and pepper to the skillet, tossing gently to combine with vegetables. Transfer the mixture to a serving bowl and sprinkle with chives. Serve immediately. Makes 4 servings.

PER SERVING		DAILY GOAL	
Calories	240	2,000 (F), 2,500 (M)	
Total Fat	4 g	60 g or less (F), 70 g or less (M)	
Saturated fat	1 g	20 g or less (F), 23 g or less (M)	
Cholesterol	0 mg	300 mg or less	
Sodium	535 mg	2,400 mg or less	
Carbohydrates	45 g	250 g or more	
Protein	12 g	55 g to 90 g	

40

VEGETABLE LASAGNA

You can indulge in lasagna if you're careful about what you put in it. This version is topped with plenty of veggies and part-skim cheeses.

▽ *Low-calorie*
  Prep time: 40 to 45 minutes
  Cooking time: 30 to 40 minutes
○ *Degree of difficulty: easy*

  2 teaspoons vegetable oil
  3 cups diced, unpeeled eggplant
  ¾ cup chopped onions
  1 teaspoon minced garlic
  1 can (28 ounces) crushed tomatoes
  1¼ teaspoons salt, divided
  ½ teaspoon granulated sugar
  ¼ teaspoon basil
  1 pound carrots, peeled and
      shredded
  1 package (10 ounces) frozen
      chopped spinach, thawed and
      squeezed dry
  1 container (15 ounces) part-skim
      ricotta cheese
  1 cup (4 ounces) shredded part-skim
      mozzarella cheese

  1 large egg, lightly beaten
     Pinch nutmeg
  9 lasagna noodles, cooked according
      to package directions, drained
  2 tablespoons freshly grated
      Parmesan cheese

1 Heat the oil in a large nonstick skillet over medium-high heat. Add the eggplant, onions, and garlic; cook, stirring, 5 minutes. Carefully add the tomatoes, 1 teaspoon of the salt, sugar, and basil; bring to a boil. Reduce heat to low, cover, and simmer 20 minutes, until eggplant is tender.

2 Meanwhile, preheat oven to 375°F. Bring 2 quarts of water to a boil in a large saucepan. Add the carrots and cook 1 minute; drain. Combine the carrots, spinach, ricotta, mozzarella, egg, the remaining ¼ teaspoon salt, and nutmeg in a large bowl.

3 Spoon 1¼ cups eggplant sauce in a 13x9-inch baking dish. Layer with 3 lasagna noodles and half the spinach mixture, 3 more noodles and 1¾ cups sauce, then remaining spinach and noodles. Top with remaining sauce. Sprinkle with Parmesan. Bake, uncovered, 30 to 40 minutes, until hot. Makes 8 servings.

PER SERVING		DAILY GOAL
Calories	305	2,000 (F), 2,500 (M)
Total fat	10 g	60 g or less (F), 70 g or less (M)
Saturated fat	5 g	20 g or less (F), 23 g or less (M)
Cholesterol	52 mg	300 mg or less
Sodium	721 mg	2,400 mg or less
Carbohydrates	39 g	250 g or more
Protein	18 g	55 g to 90 g

NOTES

PASTA WITH BROCCOLI RABE

Broccoli rabe, an assertive, leafy green, is also called rapini, rape, and broccoletta. In Apulia, in southern Italy, it's typically combined with orrechiette ("little ears") in an anchovy sauce.

▼ *Low-fat*
▽ *Low-calorie*
   Prep time: 10 minutes
   Cooking time: 12 to 15 minutes
○ *Degree of difficulty: easy*

1 **tablespoon plus ¼ teaspoon salt, divided**
2 **bunches broccoli rabe *or* broccoli***
1 **pound orrechiette *or* medium shell pasta**
2 **tablespoons olive oil**
1 **tablespoon minced garlic**
3 **anchovy fillets, drained on paper towels and chopped**
½ **teaspoon red pepper flakes**
½ **teaspoon freshly ground pepper**

1 Bring a large pot of water and 1 tablespoon salt to a boil over high heat. Add the broccoli rabe and cook 3 minutes. Remove with a slotted spoon and coarsely chop. Add the pasta to pot and cook according to package directions.

2 Meanwhile, heat the oil in a large skillet over high heat. Add the garlic and anchovies and cook 30 seconds, until fragrant. Add broccoli rabe, ¼ teaspoon salt, red pepper flakes, and freshly ground pepper. Cook until broccoli rabe is tender, 3 minutes more.

3 Drain pasta, reserving ¼ cup cooking liquid. Toss the hot pasta and cooking liquid with the broccoli rabe mixture in a large serving bowl. Makes 6 servings.

*Quarter broccoli spears lengthwise and chop.

PER SERVING		DAILY GOAL
Calories	375	2,000 (F), 2,500 (M)
Total Fat	6 g	60 g or less (F), 70 g or less (M)
Saturated fat	1 g	20 g or less (F), 23 g or less (M)
Cholesterol	1 mg	300 mg or less
Sodium	180 mg	2,400 mg or less
Carbohydrates	65 g	250 g or more
Protein	16 g	55 g to 90 g

BROCCOLI, RICOTTA, AND SUN-DRIED TOMATO PIZZA

Better than take-out, and definitely better for you, this speedy pizza takes advantage of a ready-made pizza crust.

▼ *Low-fat*
▽ *Low-calorie*
  Prep time: 15 minutes
  Cooking time: 15 minutes
○ *Degree of difficulty: easy*

3 **cups broccoli florets**
1 **tablespoon finely chopped sun-dried tomatoes**
¾ **cup (6 ounces) part-skim ricotta cheese**
½ **teaspoon salt**
¼ **teaspoon freshly ground pepper**
⅓ **cup prepared marinara sauce**
1 **12-inch ready-made pizza crust**
¼ **teaspoon red pepper flakes**

1 Preheat oven to 450°F. Bring 1 quart salted water to a boil in a medium saucepan. Add the broccoli and cook 2 minutes. Drain broccoli in a colander, reserving 2 teaspoons cooking water. Combine the reserved cooking water and sun-dried tomatoes in a small bowl; let stand 3 minutes, until softened.

2 Combine the ricotta, salt, pepper, and softened sun-dried tomatoes. Spread the marinara sauce evenly over pizza crust. Spoon dollops of the ricotta mixture on top. Add the broccoli and sprinkle with red pepper flakes. Bake 10 minutes. Makes 8 servings.

PER SERVING		DAILY GOAL
Calories	145	2,000 (F), 2,500 (M)
Total Fat	3 g	60 g or less (F), 70 g or less (M)
Saturated fat	1 g	20 g or less (F), 23 g or less (M)
Cholesterol	7 mg	300 mg or less
Sodium	417 mg	2,400 mg or less
Carbohydrates	22 g	250 g or more
Protein	8 g	55 g to 90 g

NOTES

45

MACARONI-AND-CHEESE CAKE

This "cake" is really an elegant version of good old mac 'n' cheese. It has all the comfort you'd expect of the original plus basil and tomatoes.

▼ *Low-fat*
▽ *Low-calorie*
   Prep time: 30 minutes
   Cooking time: 25 to 35 minutes
○ *Degree of difficulty: easy*

1¼ **cups skim milk**
 1 **can (13¾ or 14½ ounces) chicken broth, defatted (see tip, page 9), or vegetable broth**
 2 **tablespoons butter or margarine**
 ½ **cup all-purpose flour**
 ½ **teaspoon salt**
 5 **tablespoons plain dry bread crumbs, divided**
 2 **cups (8 ounces) shredded part-skim mozzarella cheese**
 ⅓ **cup plus 1 tablespoon freshly grated Parmesan cheese, divided**
 1 **cup finely chopped plum tomatoes**

 ½ **cup plus 1 tablespoon julienned fresh basil leaves or ½ cup chopped fresh parsley plus ½ teaspoon dried basil, divided**
 ¼ **teaspoon freshly ground pepper**
    Pinch ground red pepper
 3 **cups elbow macaroni, cooked according to package directions, drained**
 1 **teaspoon butter or margarine, melted**
 1 **cup seeded thinly sliced tomatoes**

1 Bring the milk and broth to a boil in a medium saucepan. Melt the 2 tablespoons butter in a large saucepan over medium heat. Add the flour and cook, whisking, 1 minute. Gradually whisk in hot milk mixture and salt and bring to a boil, whisking. Reduce heat and simmer, stirring, 3 minutes.

2 Preheat oven to 375°F. Grease a 9-inch springform pan and sprinkle with 2 tablespoons of the bread crumbs; shake out excess.

3 Stir the mozzarella, the ⅓ cup Parmesan, chopped tomatoes, ½ cup of the basil, black pepper, and red pepper into the white sauce. Stir in the cooked macaroni and spoon into prepared pan.

4 Combine the 1 teaspoon melted butter with the remaining 3 tablespoons crumbs and the remaining 1 tablespoon Parmesan in a small bowl. Sprinkle crumb mixture over macaroni. Place the pan on a cookie sheet and bake 25 to 35 minutes, until golden and bubbly. Cool 20 minutes. Garnish with tomato slices and the remaining 1 tablespoon basil. Remove the sides of the pan. Makes 8 servings.

PER SERVING		DAILY GOAL
Calories	350	2,000 (F), 2,500 (M)
Total Fat	11 g	60 g or less (F), 70 g or less (M)
Saturated fat	6 g	20 g or less (F), 23 g or less (M)
Cholesterol	31 mg	300 mg or less
Sodium	718 mg	2,400 mg or less
Carbohydrates	44 g	250 g or more
Protein	17 g	55 g to 90 g

MEDITERRANEAN PIZZA WITH FENNEL

▼ *Low-fat*
▽ *Low-calorie*
   Prep time: 20 minutes
   Cooking time: 17 minutes
○ *Degree of difficulty: easy*

 2 **teaspoons olive oil**
 1 **cup sliced onions**
 ½ **teaspoon basil**

½ teaspoon salt
1 cup sliced fennel bulb (anise)
2 tablespoons water
1 teaspoon minced garlic
¼ teaspoon fennel seed
⅓ cup prepared marinara sauce
4 ounces thinly sliced part-skim
    mozzarella cheese
1 12-inch ready-made pizza crust
1 tablespoon chopped fresh parsley

1 Preheat oven to 450°F. Heat oil in a medium skillet over medium heat. Add onions, basil, and salt. Cook, stirring frequently 5 minutes, until onions are tender. Stir in the fennel bulb, water, garlic, and fennel seed and cook 2 minutes more.

2 Spread the marinara sauce evenly over prepared pizza crust. Layer the top with the mozzarella, then the fennel-onion mixture. Bake 10 minutes. Sprinkle top with parsley. Makes 8 servings.

PER SERVING		DAILY GOAL
Calories	155	2,000 (F), 2,500 (M)
Total Fat	5 g	60 g or less (F), 70 g or less (M)
Saturated fat	2 g	20 g or less (F), 23 g or less (M)
Cholesterol	8 mg	300 mg or less
Sodium	456 mg	2,400 mg or less
Carbohydrates	20 g	250 g or more
Protein	7 g	55 g to 90 g

SALAD SOLUTION

A salad of crisp mixed greens is one of the best ways we know of to round out a healthful meal. You won't waste any of your daily fat allowance with these zesty dressings, and they're so rich tasting, you'll never miss the fat.

Creamy Dijon Dressing: In a medium bowl, blend 1 container (8 ounces) plain nonfat yogurt, 1 tablespoon fresh lemon juice, 2 teaspoons whole-grain Dijon mustard, ½ teaspoon salt, and ¼ teaspoon freshly ground pepper until smooth. Makes 1 cup.

PER TABLESPOON		DAILY GOAL
Calories	10	2,000 (F), 2,500 (M)
Total Fat	0 g	60 g or less (F), 70 g or less (M)
Saturated fat	0 g	20 g or less (F), 23 g or less (M)
Cholesterol	0 mg	300 mg or less
Sodium	98 mg	2,400 mg or less
Carbohydrates	1 g	250 g or more
Protein	1 g	55 g to 90 g

Tarragon Tofu Dressing: Warm ¼ cup tarragon vinegar in a small saucepan over low heat. Add 1 tablespoon sugar and heat until dissolved; cool. In a blender, combine 8 ounces soft tofu, ½ cup buttermilk, and 2 tablespoons fresh lemon juice and blend until smooth. Through the hole in the blender cover, add 1 tablespoon chopped fresh tarragon, 1 teaspoon salt, ½ teaspoon dry mustard, and the vinegar mixture. Blend until smooth. Makes 2 cups.

PER TABLESPOON		DAILY GOAL
Calories	10	2,000 (F), 2,500 (M)
Total Fat	.2 g	60 g or less (F), 70 g or less (M)
Saturated fat	0 g	20 g or less (F), 23 g or less (M)
Cholesterol	0 mg	300 mg or less
Sodium	73 mg	2,400 mg or less

Southwest Yogurt Dressing: In a blender, combine 1 container (8 ounces) plain nonfat yogurt; 1 tablespoon low-fat sour cream; 1 can (4 ounces) chopped green chiles, drained; 1 tablespoon chopped fresh parsley; ¼ teaspoon each cumin and ground coriander; ⅛ teaspoon each salt and freshly ground pepper; and a pinch of chili powder. Blend until smooth. Makes 1⅓ cups.

PER TABLESPOON		DAILY GOAL
Calories	10	2,000 (F), 2,500 (M)
Total Fat	0 g	60 g or less (F), 70 g or less (M)
Saturated fat	0 g	20 g or less (F), 23 g or less (M)
Cholesterol	0 mg	300 mg or less
Sodium	55 mg	2,400 mg or less
Carbohydrates	1 g	250 g or more
Protein	1 g	55 g to 90 g

RICOTTA AND VEGETABLE QUICHE

Who needs a pastry crust when you can sink your teeth into this luscious cheese pie packed with potatoes, asparagus, spinach, and a touch of lemon? If you can't find light ricotta cheese, simply substitute 1 cup each part-skim and nonfat cheeses.

Ⓜ *Microwave*
▽ *Low-calorie*
   Prep time: 25 minutes
   Cooking time: 14 to 17 minutes
◯ *Degree of difficulty: easy*

- 8 ounces asparagus, trimmed and cut into ½-inch pieces
- 1 container (15 ounces) light ricotta cheese
- ¼ cup low-fat (1%) milk
- 2 large egg yolks
- 1 tablespoon cornstarch
- 1 teaspoon salt
- ¼ teaspoon freshly ground pepper
- ¼ teaspoon grated lemon peel
- ¼ cup (1 ounce) shredded part-skim mozzarella cheese
- ¼ cup freshly grated Parmesan cheese
- 1 package (10 ounces) frozen chopped spinach, thawed and squeezed dry
- 2 cups diced cooked potatoes
- 3 large egg whites
- 1 tablespoon butter *or* margarine

1 Preheat oven to 400°F. Combine the asparagus and 1 tablespoon of water in a 9-inch glass pie plate. Cover with wax paper and microwave on high (100% power) 2 to 3 minutes, until just tender. Drain and set aside.

2 Whisk together the ricotta, milk, egg yolks, cornstarch, salt, pepper, and lemon peel until smooth. Stir in the mozzarella and Parmesan cheeses. Then add the asparagus, spinach, and potatoes and stir until well combined.

3 Beat the egg whites in a small mixing bowl at medium-high speed until stiff. Fold the egg whites into the ricotta mixture with a rubber spatula.

4 Melt the butter in a 10-inch nonstick skillet over medium-high heat. Remove skillet from heat. Wrap the skillet handle with foil. Spoon ricotta mixture into the pan. Return to heat and cook, without stirring, 1 minute. Transfer the quiche to the oven and bake 12 to 14 minutes, until the center is set. To remove the quiche, cut around the edge then invert the pan onto a serving plate. Makes 6 servings.

PER SERVING		DAILY GOAL	
Calories	235	2,000 (F), 2,500 (M)	
Total Fat	10 g	60 g or less (F), 70 g or less (M)	
Saturated fat	5 g	20 g or less (F), 23 g or less (M)	
Cholesterol	90 mg	300 mg or less	
Sodium	647 mg	2,400 mg or less	
Carbohydrates	18 g	250 g or more	
Protein	19 g	55 g to 90 g	

NOTES

RATATOUILLE OMELET

A classic savory omelet like this one can be enjoyed any time of day—as part of a hearty breakfast, lunch, or light supper. The filling is completely do-ahead and can be refrigerated up to three days or frozen up to a month. Just measure the amount of filling you need and whip up as many omelets as you please.

▼ *Low-calorie*
▽ *Prep time: 20 minutes*
   Cooking time: 55 minutes
○ *Degree of difficulty: easy*

Ratatouille Filling
- 1 unpeeled eggplant (about 1 pound), finely diced
- 2½ teaspoons salt, divided
- 1 tablespoon olive oil
- 3 cups finely diced onions
- 3½ cups finely diced zucchini
- 1 cup finely diced red pepper
- ¾ cup diced green pepper
- 4 garlic cloves, minced
- 1 can (14½ *or* 16 ounces) tomatoes in puree
- ½ teaspoon freshly ground pepper
- ½ teaspoon thyme

Omelet
- 1 large egg
- 2 large egg whites
- ⅛ teaspoon salt

1 For Ratatouille Filling, combine the eggplant and 2 teaspoons of the salt in a large colander. Drain 20 minutes; pat dry with paper towels.

2 Heat the oil in a large saucepan over medium-high heat. Add the onions and cook until tender, about 5 minutes. Stir in the eggplant, the remaining ½ teaspoon salt, zucchini, red and green peppers, garlic, tomatoes, ground pepper, and thyme. Reduce heat and simmer, partially covered, about 45 minutes, until vegetables are tender. Makes 6 cups.

3 For Omelet, whisk together egg, egg whites, and salt in a medium bowl until frothy. Spray a medium nonstick skillet with vegetable cooking spray and heat over medium-low heat. Pour the eggs into the pan. When eggs begin to set, spread ½ cup of the Ratatouille Filling on top and continue to cook until the bottom begins to brown. Gently fold the omelet in half and turn onto a serving plate. Makes 1 serving.

Note: For additional omelets, wipe skillet clean with paper towels and repeat process with another recipe of egg mixture and ½ cup Ratatouille Filling.

PER SERVING		DAILY GOAL
Calories	170	2,000 (F), 2,500 (M)
Total Fat	7 g	60 g or less (F), 70 g or less (M)
Saturated fat	2 g	20 g or less (F), 23 g or less (M)
Cholesterol	212 mg	300 mg or less
Sodium	785 mg	2,400 mg or less
Carbohydrates	12 g	250 g or more
Protein	15 g	55 g to 90 g

NOTES

49

CURRIED VEGETABLE STRUDEL

▼ *Low-fat*
Prep time: 50 minutes plus cooling
Cooking time: 1½ hours
◒ *Degree of difficulty: moderate*

Yellow Dal

   3 **cups water**
  ¾ **cup yellow split peas**
  ¼ **cup finely chopped celery**
   1 **large clove garlic, smashed**
   1 **teaspoon cumin**
  ½ **teaspoon salt**
  ⅛ **teaspoon turmeric**

Vegetable Strudel

   4 **teaspoons vegetable oil, divided**
   1 **cup minced onions**
   1 **teaspoon minced garlic**
   1 **teaspoon minced fresh ginger**
   1 **teaspoon curry powder**
  ½ **teaspoon cumin**
  ⅛ **teaspoon ground red pepper (optional)**
   2 **pounds diced all-purpose potatoes**
  1½ **cups water**

  1¼ **teaspoons salt**
   1 **cup diced carrots**
   1 **cup tiny cauliflower florets**
   1 **cup frozen peas**
  ¼ **cup chopped fresh cilantro**
   5 **sheets phyllo dough**
   4 **teaspoons plain dry bread crumbs**

   1 **container (8 ounces) plain nonfat yogurt**
  ¼ **teaspoon grated lime peel**

1 For Yellow Dal, bring the water to a boil in a large saucepan. Stir in the split peas, celery, garlic, cumin, salt, and turmeric. Return to a boil. Cover and simmer 1¼ hours, until peas are very tender. Beat or whisk until smooth.

2 Meanwhile, for Vegetable Strudel, heat 1 teaspoon of the oil in a large skillet over medium heat. Add the onions and cook, stirring 7 to 10 minutes, until tender. Stir in the minced garlic, ginger, curry, cumin, and red pepper; cook 30 seconds. Stir in the potatoes and cook 2 minutes. Stir in water and salt. Bring to a boil. Reduce heat; cover and simmer 10 minutes. Add the carrots and cauliflower; simmer, covered, 10 minutes more, until tender. Uncover and simmer until no longer soupy, if

necessary. Stir in the peas and cilantro. (Can be made ahead. Cover and refrigerate up to 24 hours.)

3 Preheat oven to 400°F. Spread 1 sheet of phyllo dough on an ungreased cookie sheet. (Keep remaining phyllo covered with plastic wrap.) Brush lightly with some of the remaining 3 teaspoons oil, and sprinkle with 1 teaspoon of the bread crumbs. Continue layering remaining phyllo on top, brushing each sheet with oil and sprinkling with crumbs.

4 Spoon the vegetable mixture down the center of one long side of phyllo. Fold one side of phyllo over and tuck under filling. Roll phyllo log so that the seam side is down. Brush with any remaining oil. With a sharp knife, score the top of the strudel diagonally at 1½-inch intervals. Bake 20 minutes, until golden.

5 Combine yogurt and lime peel in a small bowl. Serve the hot strudel with Yellow Dal and yogurt-lime mixture.

PER SERVING		DAILY GOAL	
Calories	525	2,000 (F), 2,500 (M)	
Total Fat	7 g	60 g or less (F), 70 g or less (M)	
Saturated fat	1 g	20 g or less (F), 23 g or less (M)	
Cholesterol	1 mg	300 mg or less	
Sodium	1,219 mg	2,400 mg or less	
Carbohydrates	96 g	250 g or more	
Protein	22 g	55 g to 90 g	

SUMMER GARDEN PASTA

▼ *Low-fat*
▽ *Low-calorie*
   Prep time: 10 minutes
   Cooking time: 20 minutes
○ *Degree of difficulty: easy*

  4 **large tomatoes, chopped**
 ¼ **cup freshly grated Parmesan cheese**
  2 **tablespoons chopped fresh dill**
  4 **tablespoons olive oil, divided**
  1 **teaspoon salt, divided**
 ¼ **teaspoon freshly ground pepper**
 ½ **cup chopped onion**
  2 **small zucchini, halved lengthwise and sliced ¼ inch thick**
  1 **teaspoon minced garlic**
 ¼ **cup dry white wine**
  1 **pound bow-tie pasta, cooked according to package directions, drained**

1 Combine the tomatoes, Parmesan, dill, 2 tablespoons of the oil, ½ teaspoon of the salt, and the pepper in a large bowl.

2 Heat the remaining 2 tablespoons oil in a large skillet over medium-high heat. Add the onion and cook, stirring, until onion is tender and beginning to brown, 8 to 10 minutes. Stir in the zucchini and cook 4 to 5 minutes, until golden. Add the garlic and the remaining ½ teaspoon salt and cook 1 minute. Add the wine; bring to a boil and cook 1 minute more.

3 Stir the hot pasta and zucchini mixture into the tomatoes. Toss well. Makes 6 servings.

PER SERVING		DAILY GOAL
Calories	420	2,000 (F), 2,500 (M)
Total fat	12 g	60 g or less (F), 70 g or less (M)
Saturated fat	2 g	20 g or less (F), 23 g or less (M)
Cholesterol	3 mg	300 mg or less
Sodium	642 mg	2,400 mg or less
Carbohydrates	64 g	250 g or more
Protein	13 g	55 g to 90 g

WINTER VEGETABLE STEW

▼ *Low-fat*
▽ *Low-calorie*
   Prep time: 35 minutes
   Cooking time: 50 to 55 minutes
○ *Degree of difficulty: easy*

  3 **tablespoons olive oil**
1½ **tablespoons curry powder**
  2 **cups chopped leeks (white part only)**
  6 **medium carrots, peeled and cut into 1-inch pieces**
  4 **medium celery ribs, cut diagonally into 1-inch pieces**
  4 **all-purpose potatoes (1¼ pounds), peeled and cut into 1-inch pieces**
  3 **medium white turnips (10 ounces) peeled and cut into 1-inch pieces**
  1 **medium butternut squash (1½ pounds), peeled and cut into 1-inch pieces**
1½ **teaspoons savory *or* ½ teaspoon thyme**
  1 **teaspoon salt**
  1 **bay leaf**
  2 **cans (13¾ *or* 14½ ounces each) chicken broth, defatted (see tip, page 9), *or* vegetable broth**
  1 **cup water**
2½ **cups small cauliflower florets**
1½ **cups frozen peas**

1 Heat the oil in a large Dutch oven over medium-high heat. Add the curry powder and cook, stirring, 1 minute. Add the leeks, carrots, and celery. Cook, stirring frequently, until the vegetables begin to brown, 10 minutes. Add the potatoes and turnips; cook, stirring occasionally, 5 minutes more. Add the squash, savory, salt, and bay leaf and cook 5 minutes.

2 Stir the chicken broth and water into the vegetable mixture. Bring to a boil. Reduce heat and simmer, uncovered, 10 minutes. Remove the bay leaf. (Can be made ahead. Spoon into freezer containers. Cover and freeze up to 1 month; reheat.)

3 Add the cauliflower and peas and simmer until all the vegetables are tender, 15 to 20 minutes. Makes 12 cups.

PER SERVING		DAILY GOAL
Calories	145	2,000 (F), 2,500 (M)
Total Fat	4 g	60 g or less (F), 70 g or less (M)
Saturated fat	.5 g	20 g or less (F), 23 g or less (M)
Cholesterol	0 mg	300 mg or less
Sodium	593 mg	2,400 mg or less
Carbohydrates	24 g	250 g or more
Protein	4 g	55 g to 90 g

HARVEST VEGETABLE SOUP

Here's a hearty soup from cookbook author Richard Olney, a noted authority on French food and wine. In keeping with the seasons, he adds fresh little peas in the spring or cut-up ripe tomatoes in August.

The soup should be thick, and the pasta should be well done, not al dente.

▼ *Low-fat*
▽ *Low-calorie*
   Prep time: 30 minutes
   Cooking time: 50 to 55 minutes
○ *Degree of difficulty: easy*

6 cups water
1 sprig fresh thyme *or* ¼ teaspoon
      dried thyme
1 bay leaf
2 teaspoons kosher salt *or*
      1½ teaspoons table salt
1 small head garlic, cloves separated,
      peeled, and crushed
      (about ⅓ cup)
1½ cups carrots, cut into ¼-inch dice
3 cups thinly sliced leeks
      (white part only)
2½ cups diced onions
1¾ cups diced (½ inch) all-purpose
      potatoes
2½ cups zucchini, quartered
      lengthwise and sliced ½ inch
      thick
1¼ cups broken up spaghetti *or* short
      macaroni
1 cup green beans, trimmed and cut
      into ¼-inch pieces
4 teaspoons butter, cut up

Freshly grated Parmesan cheese
(optional)
Freshly ground pepper (optional)

1 Combine the water, thyme, bay leaf, salt, and garlic in a large Dutch oven. Bring to a boil over medium-high heat. Add the carrots and return to a boil. Reduce heat and simmer, partially covered, 5 minutes. Repeat the process with leeks, then onions, then potatoes, then zucchini, simmering 5 minutes after each addition.

2 Return the soup to a boil. Add the pasta and cook, covered, stirring occasionally, 8 minutes. Add the green beans and cook until vegetables are tender and soup is thick, 7 to 8 minutes more. Discard bay leaf.

3 Ladle the soup into warmed soup bowls. Top each with ½ teaspoon butter. Serve with Parmesan and pepper, if desired. Makes 10 cups.

PER CUP WITHOUT PARMESAN		DAILY GOAL
Calories	145	2,000 (F), 2,500 (M)
Total fat	2 g	60 g or less (F), 70 g or less (M)
Saturated fat	1 g	20 g or less (F), 23 g or less (M)
Cholesterol	4 mg	300 mg or less
Sodium	329 mg	2,400 mg or less
Carbohydrates	29 g	250 g or more
Protein	4 g	55 g to 90 g

53

TRIPLE POTATO CHOWDER

You can make this soup with just one type of potato, but we used three—red, purple, and yellow—as a treat for the eye as well as the palate.

▼ *Low-fat*
▽ *Low-calorie*
   Prep time: 35 minutes
   Cooking time: 25 to 30 minutes
○ *Degree of difficulty: easy*

1 tablespoon butter *or* margarine
1½ cups diced, well-rinsed leeks
1 cup diced celery
1 cup diced carrots
1 teaspoon minced garlic
1½ cups diced, unpeeled red new
      potatoes
1½ cups diced, unpeeled purple
      potatoes
1½ cups diced, unpeeled yellow
      potatoes

2 cans (13¾ *or* 14½ ounces each)
      chicken broth, defatted (see tip,
      page 9) plus enough water to
      equal 5 cups
   Pinch thyme
½ of 1 bay leaf
¼ teaspoon freshly ground pepper
2 tablespoons minced fresh parsley

1 Melt the butter in a large saucepan over medium heat. Add the leeks, celery, carrot, and garlic. Cook 5 minutes, until the vegetables have softened. Add the red, purple, and yellow potatoes; chicken broth; water; thyme; bay leaf; and pepper.

2 Bring the soup to a boil. Reduce heat and simmer, partially covered, 20 to 25 minutes, until potatoes are tender. Remove the bay leaf and stir in the parsley. Makes 6 cups.

PER CUP		DAILY GOAL
Calories	165	2,000 (F), 2,500 (M)
Total Fat	4 g	60 g or less (F), 70 g or less (M)
Saturated fat	1 g	20 g or less (F), 23 g or less (M)
Cholesterol	5 mg	300 mg or less
Sodium	1,023 mg	2,400 mg or less
Carbohydrates	28 g	250 g or more
Protein	4 g	55 g to 90 g

SMOKY VEGETABLE CHILI

The robust flavor of this meatless chili comes from the chipotle chiles, jalapeños that have been smoked.

▼   *Low-fat*
▽   *Low-calorie*
    Prep time: 30 minutes plus soaking
    Cooking time: 1¾ hours
○   *Degree of difficulty: easy*

1½ **cups dried black beans**
1½ **cups dried small red beans**
 2 **dried pasilla *or* ancho chiles**
    Water
 2 **dried chipotle chiles *or* 1 can
    (7 ounces) chipotle chiles
    in adobo***
 1 **tablespoon vegetable oil**
 3 **cups chopped onions**
 1 **green pepper, diced**
 1 **red pepper, diced**
 1 **tablespoon cumin**
 1 **tablespoon minced garlic**
 2 **dried árbol *or* serrano chiles**

 1 **can (14½ *or* 16 ounces) tomatoes,
    chopped with their liquid**
 1 **large butternut squash, peeled and
    cut into ¾-inch dice (5 cups)**
 1 **tablespoon salt**
 1 **package (10 ounces) frozen lima
    beans**
    **Plain yogurt, lime wedges, and
    flour tortillas**

1   Rinse black and red beans and pick over for small stones and shriveled beans. In a large bowl, cover beans with 2 inches water and soak overnight. (To quick-soak: Combine beans and water to cover 2 inches in a large saucepan and bring to a boil; boil 2 minutes. Cover and let stand 1 hour.) Drain in a colander; set aside.

2   Heat a large cast-iron skillet over medium-low heat. Remove the stems and seeds from the pasilla chiles and dried chipotle, if using. Toast chiles, turning frequently, until fragrant and pliable, 2 minutes. (Be careful of the peppery smoke.)

3   Transfer chiles to a blender. Bring ½ cup water to a boil. Add the water to chiles and purée until smooth. Set aside. (For chipotles in adobo, purée them in a

clean blender until smooth. Reserve 2 tablespoons. Refrigerate remaining purée for another use.)

4   Heat the oil in a large Dutch oven over medium-high heat. Add the onions and red and green peppers and cook 10 minutes. Stir in the cumin, garlic, and árbol chiles; cook 30 seconds. Add the drained beans, pasilla purée, reserved chipotle-in-adobo purée (if using) and 6½ cups water. Bring to a boil, cover, and simmer 1 hour, until beans are almost tender.

5   Stir in the tomatoes and their liquid, squash, and salt; return to a boil. Reduce heat, cover, and cook 10 minutes. Add the lima beans and cook 20 minutes more. Remove árbol chiles. Serve with dollops of yogurt, lime wedges, and tortillas. Makes 15 cups.

PER CUP SERVING WITH 1 TORTILLA		DAILY GOAL
Calories	365	2,000 (F), 2,500 (M)
Total Fat	3 g	60 g or less (F), 70 g or less (M)
Saturated fat	1 g	20 g or less (F), 23 g or less (M)
Cholesterol	2 mg	300 mg or less
Sodium	797 mg	2,400 mg or less
Carbohydrates	70 g	250 g or more
Protein	17 g	55 g to 90 g

BLACK BEAN CHILI

This hearty chili can be prepared with black or pinto beans. Serve it in bowls over nutty brown rice and top with a dollop of yogurt and cilantro sprigs. Sliced ripe tomatoes with red onion makes a simple side dish.

▼ *Low-fat*
▽ *Low-calorie*
    Prep time: 10 minutes plus soaking
    Cooking time: 2 ½ hours
○ *Degree of difficulty: easy*

1 **pound dried black *or* pinto beans**
1 **tablespoon olive oil**
2 **cups chopped onions**
1 **cup chopped carrots**
3 **tablespoons chili powder**
1 **tablespoon minced garlic**
1 **teaspoon cumin**
½ **to 1 teaspoon red pepper flakes**
¼ **teaspoon cinnamon**
3 **cans (13¾ *or* 14½ ounces each) low-sodium chicken broth, defatted (see tip, page 9) *or* vegetable broth**
2 **cups water**
2 **teaspoons oregano**
1 **teaspoon salt**
3 **cups hot cooked brown rice Plain nonfat yogurt and cilantro sprigs, for garnish**

1 Rinse the beans and pick them over for small stones and shriveled beans. In a large bowl, cover beans with 2 inches water and soak overnight. (To quick-soak: Combine beans and water to cover 2 inches in a large saucepan and bring to a boil; boil 2 minutes. Cover and let stand 1 hour.) Drain in a colander; set aside.

2 Heat the oil in a large Dutch oven over medium heat. Add the onions and carrots and cook 10 minutes, stirring frequently, until vegetables have softened. Add the chili powder, garlic, cumin, red pepper flakes, and cinnamon; cook, stirring, 1 minute. Add the beans, chicken broth, water, oregano, and salt and bring to a boil. Reduce heat and simmer, partially covered, 2 hours, until beans are tender.

3 With a slotted spoon, transfer 2 cups of beans to a medium bowl and mash with a potato masher until lumpy. Return the mashed beans to remaining chili, stirring until blended. Serve chili over ½ cup cooked brown rice and garnish with yogurt and cilantro. Makes 6 servings.

PER SERVING WITH 1/2 CUP RICE		DAILY GOAL
Calories	450	2,000 (F), 2,500 (M)
Total Fat	6 g	60 g or less (F), 70 g or less (M)
Saturated fat	1 g	20 g or less (F), 23 g or less (M)
Cholesterol	0 mg	300 mg or less
Sodium	458 mg	2,400 mg or less
Carbohydrates	80 g	250 g or more
Protein	22 g	55 g to 90 g

NOTES

SIMPLY

SEAFOOD

For centuries, cooks have capitalized on the splendors from the sea—the vast selection of fish and shellfish, many low in fat and calories. Varieties that were once difficult to find are now widely available. So, try something new. You'll love our Halibut with Warm Tomato Salsa. To make an impression with guests, serve vibrant Shrimp-Couscous Salad with Carrot-Ginger Vinaigrette. Every recipe is a prize catch!

SALMON WITH CITRUS VINAIGRETTE AND LENTILS

You won't have to sacrifice time or fat grams with this trendy combination of seafood and legumes that will impress friends and family with its sophisticated taste.

▼ *Low-fat*
   Prep time: 30 minutes
   Cookinging time: 8 to 10 minutes
⊖ *Degree of difficulty: moderate*

1 **cup lentils, rinsed and picked over**
2 **cups water**
1 **teaspoon salt, divided**
6 **teaspoons olive oil, divided**
⅓ **cup minced shallots**
¼ **cup chopped fresh parsley**
1 **tablespoon fresh lemon juice**
1 **tablespoon fresh orange juice**
½ **teaspoon grated lemon peel**
½ **teaspoon grated orange peel**
¼ **teaspoon freshly ground pepper**
1 **pound salmon fillet, cut into
   4 pieces**
   Watercress, for garnish

1 Combine the lentils, water, and ½ teaspoon of the salt in a medium saucepan. Bring to a boil. Reduce heat and simmer until lentils are just tender, 20 to 25 minutes. Drain the lentils and keep warm.

2 Heat 2 teaspoons of the oil in a small saucepan over medium-high heat. Add the shallots and cook 2 minutes. Stir shallots into lentils and add parsley. Cover.

3 Meanwhile, for vinaigrette, whisk together the lemon juice, orange juice, lemon peel, orange peel, the remaining 4 teaspoons olive oil, the remaining ½ teaspoon salt, and pepper together until combined.

4 Preheat broiler. Line a broiler pan with foil and place the salmon on top. Drizzle 1 teaspoon of the citrus vinaigrette over each piece. Broil the salmon 4 inches from heat source 8 to 10 minutes, until the fish is opaque in center.

5 Spoon the lentils onto a platter and top with salmon fillets. Drizzle the top with remaining vinaigrette and garnish with watercress, if desired. Makes 4 servings.

PER SERVING		DAILY GOAL
Calories	395	2,000 (F), 2,500 (M)
Total Fat	14 g	60 g or less (F), 70 g or less (M)
Saturated fat	2 g	20 g or less (F), 23 g or less (M)
Cholesterol	62 mg	300 mg or less
Sodium	605 mg	2,400 mg or less
Carbohydrates	31 g	250 g or more
Protein	36 g	55 g to 90 g

NOTES

WARM TUNA SALAD

The potatoes are microwaved and the fish is pan-broiled in just a little olive oil. Topped with a warm dressing, this salad has everything, except a lot of fat.

Ⓜ *Microwave*
▼ *Low-fat*
▽ *Low-calorie*
   Prep time: 25 minutes
   Cooking time: 10 minutes
○ *Degree of difficulty: easy*

1 **pound red new potatoes,
     thinly sliced
   Water**
1 **tablespoon drained capers**
1 **bunch (12 ounces) fresh spinach,
     stems removed and washed**
1 **head radicchio, torn (3 cups)
   Salt
   Freshly ground pepper**
1 **pound tuna *or* swordfish steak,
     1 inch thick, cut into 4 pieces**
2 **teaspoons plus 1 tablespoon
     balsamic vinegar, divided**
2 **teaspoons olive oil, divided**
½ **cup sliced shallots**

½ **teaspoon minced garlic**
½ **cup chicken broth, defatted
     (see tip, page 9)
   Pinch thyme**

1 Combine the potatoes, 2 tablespoons of water, and ¼ teaspoon salt in a 1-quart microwave-proof casserole. Cover and microwave on high (100% power) 10 minutes, stirring once halfway through, until tender. Stir in the capers; cover and keep warm.

2 Meanwhile, place the spinach and radicchio in a large bowl. Combine ¼ teaspoon salt and ¼ teaspoon pepper in a cup. Brush the tuna on both sides with 2 teaspoons of the vinegar, then sprinkle it with the salt and pepper mixture.

3 Heat 1 teaspoon of the oil in a large nonstick skillet over medium-high heat. Add tuna and cook 2½ to 3 minutes per side for medium doneness. Transfer tuna to a plate.

4 Add the remaining 1 teaspoon oil and the shallots to the skillet and cook, stirring, 2 minutes. Stir in the remaining 1 tablespoon vinegar and the garlic; cook until syrupy. Add the chicken broth, thyme, ¼ teaspoon salt, and ¼ teaspoon pepper; bring to a boil.

5 Pour warm dressing over greens and toss. Arrange greens on 4 plates. Top each plate with tuna and potatoes. Makes 4 servings.

PER SERVING		DAILY GOAL
Calories	320	2,000 (F), 2,500 (M)
Total Fat	9 g	60 g or less (F), 70 g or less (M)
Saturated fat	2 g	20 g or less (F), 23 g or less (M)
Cholesterol	43 mg	300 mg or less
Sodium	735 mg	2,400 mg or less
Carbohydrates	29 g	250 g or more
Protein	32 g	55 g to 90 g

NOTES

61

GINGER-GLAZED SALMON WITH RICE

For this elegant entrée, the fish can be marinated ahead or just before cooking. The glaze is a compelling combination of sweet, salty, and tart flavors. *Also pictured on page 58.*

▼ *Low-fat*
  Prep time: 20 minutes
  Cooking time: 20 minutes
○ *Degree of difficulty: easy*

   2 **tablespoons chopped fresh mint, divided**
   1 **tablespoon soy sauce**
   1 **tablespoon fresh lime juice**
   1½ **teaspoons firmly packed brown sugar**
   ½ **teaspoon grated lime peel**
   ½ **teaspoon grated fresh ginger**
   ¼ **teaspoon freshly ground pepper**
   1½ **pounds salmon fillet, skinned and cut into 4 pieces, *or* 4 salmon steaks**
   1 **cup long-grain rice**
   ½ **cup frozen peas, thawed**
   ½ **cup frozen whole-kernel corn, thawed**
   ¼ **cup sliced green onions**
   2 **tablespoons chopped fresh cilantro**

1 For ginger glaze, combine 1 tablespoon of the mint, soy sauce, lime juice, brown sugar, lime peel, ginger, and pepper in a shallow dish. Add the salmon, turning to coat pieces with the glaze. (Can be made ahead. Cover and refrigerate up to 24 hours.)

2 For rice pilaf, cook the rice according to package directions. Fluff the rice with a fork. Stir in the peas, corn, green onions, cilantro, and the remaining 1 tablespoon mint.

3 Preheat broiler. Line a jelly-roll pan with foil. Arrange the salmon on the prepared pan and spoon glaze on top. Broil the fish 4 inches from the heat source without turning it, 8 to 10 minutes, until the fish is opaque. Let stand 5 minutes. Serve the salmon on a bed of rice pilaf. Makes 4 servings.

PER SERVING		DAILY GOAL
Calories	455	2,000 (F), 2,500 (M)
Total Fat	11 g	60 g or less (F), 70 g or less (M)
Saturated fat	2 g	20 g or less (F), 23 g or less (M)
Cholesterol	94 mg	300 mg or less
Sodium	357 mg	2,400 mg or less
Carbohydrates	47 g	250 g or more
Protein	39 g	55 g to 90 g

NOTES

SNAPPER LIVORNESE

In Livorno, a busy Tuscan port city, fish such as snapper or mullet is served with tomatoes, garlic, and parsley. A touch of chopped olives adds an extra kick of flavor to this recipe.

▼ *Low-fat*
▽ *Low-calorie*
   Prep time: 30 minutes
   Cooking time: 15 to 20 minutes
○ *Degree of difficulty: easy*

2	**tablespoons olive oil, divided**
¼	**cup finely chopped onion**
4	**tablespoons chopped fresh parsley, divided**
1	**tablespoon minced garlic**
	Pinch red pepper flakes
1	**can (14½ or 16 ounces) tomatoes, with their liquid**
	Salt
	Freshly ground pepper
1½	**pounds red snapper fillets**
¼	**cup all-purpose flour**
1	**tablespoon butter or margarine**
¼	**cup pitted, coarsely chopped Gaeta or green Sicilian olives**

1 Heat 1 tablespoon of the oil in a medium skillet over medium heat. Add the onion, 2 tablespoons of the parsley, garlic, and pepper flakes. Cook, stirring, 5 minutes, until onion is tender. Add the tomatoes with their liquid and ⅛ teaspoon salt. Cook, breaking up tomatoes with a spoon, 15 minutes, until thick.

2 Sprinkle the fish with salt and pepper. Spread the flour on a sheet of wax paper. Dip both sides of fish in flour, shaking off the excess.

3 Heat the remaining 1 tablespoon oil with the butter in a large nonstick skillet over medium-high heat. Add fish in batches and cook until golden, 3 minutes per side. Stir in the olives and the remaining 2 tablespoons parsley into sauce. Serve sauce with fish. Makes 4 servings.

PER SERVING		DAILY GOAL
Calories	320	2,000 (F), 2,500 (M)
Total fat	13 g	60 g or less (F), 70 g or less (M)
Saturated fat	3 g	20 g or less (F), 23 g or less (M)
Cholesterol	71 mg	300 mg or less
Sodium	376 mg	2,400 mg or less
Carbohydrates	13 g	250 g or more
Protein	37 g	55 g to 90 g

NOTES

CITRUS COD WITH FENNEL AND POTATOES

Everything in this healthy, fresh-tasting meal is cooked in the same dish and is on the table in thirty minutes. The cod is perfect with a mixed green salad and any of our fabulous lean dressings (see tip, page 47).

Ⓜ *Microwave*
▼ *Low-fat*
▽ *Low-calorie*
   Prep time: 15 minutes
   Microwave time: 28 minutes
〇 *Degree of difficulty: easy*

1 **pound all-purpose potatoes, very thinly sliced**
1 **bulb fennel (anise), very thinly sliced**
1 **cup very thinly sliced onions**
   Salt
   Freshly ground pepper
¼ **cup chicken broth, defatted (see tip, page 9)**
1 **pound cod fillets**
2 **navel oranges, peeled and sectioned**

1 Combine the potatoes, fennel, onions, ¼ teaspoon salt, and ¼ teaspoon pepper in a shallow, 2-quart microwave-proof casserole. Drizzle the vegetables with the chicken broth. Cover with plastic wrap and microwave on high (100% power) 20 minutes, stirring once halfway through.

2 Uncover and arrange the cod on the vegetables. Sprinkle with another ¼ teaspoon salt and ⅛ teaspoon pepper. Cover with wax paper and microwave on high (100% power) 8 minutes, until fish is opaque. Transfer the fish and potato mixture to a serving plate. Garnish with oranges. Makes 4 servings.

PER SERVING		DAILY GOAL	
Calories	250	2,000 (F), 2,500 (M)	
Total fat	1 g	60 g or less (F), 70 g or less (M)	
Saturated fat	0 g	20 g or less (F), 23 g or less (M)	
Cholesterol	49 mg	300 mg or less	
Sodium	381 mg	2,400 mg or less	
Carbohydrates	35 g	250 g or more	
Protein	25 g	55 g to 90 g	

NOTES

HALIBUT WITH WARM TOMATO SALSA

This fast, flavorful fish is coated with a spicy dry rub, quickly cooked, and topped with a fresh salsa. You may also use cod fillets.

▼ *Low-fat*
▽ *Low-calorie*
   Prep time: 10 minutes
   Cooking time: 8 to 10 minutes
○ *Degree of difficulty: easy*

   1 **large tomato, cut into ½-inch dice**
   1 **tablespoon fresh lime juice**
   1 **teaspoon minced garlic**
1½ **teaspoons chili powder**
   ½ **teaspoon cumin**
   ½ **teaspoon salt**
   ¼ **teaspoon oregano**
   ¼ **teaspoon freshly ground pepper**
1½ **pounds halibut fillets, cut into
        4 pieces**
   2 **teaspoons vegetable oil**
   1 **tablespoon chopped fresh cilantro**
   8 **flour tortillas, warmed
        Lime wedges, for garnish**

1 For salsa, combine the tomato, lime juice, and garlic in a medium bowl. Set aside.

2 Combine the chili powder, cumin, salt, oregano, and pepper in a small bowl. Rub the spice mixture on both sides of the fish.

3 Heat the oil in a large nonstick skillet over medium-high heat. Add fish and cook 3 to 4 minutes per side, until just opaque in center. Transfer the fish to a platter and keep warm. Add the salsa to the pan and cook, stirring, 1 minute, until just heated through. Spoon salsa over fish and sprinkle with the cilantro. Serve with tortillas and lime wedges, if desired. Makes 4 servings.

PER SERVING		DAILY GOAL
Calories	405	2,000 (F), 2,500 (M)
Total Fat	9 g	60 g or less (F), 70 g or less (M)
Saturated fat	1 g	20 g or less (F), 23 g or less (M)
Cholesterol	73 mg	300 mg or less
Sodium	715 mg	2,400 mg or less
Carbohydrates	43 g	250 g or more
Protein	37 g	55 g to 90 g

NOTES

LEMONY SOLE WITH CAPERS AND BROCCOLI

This speedy seafood and veggie entrée needs only ½ cup cooked rice or orzo to satisfy. It's all prepared on a large plate thanks to the microwave.

Ⓜ *Microwave*
▼ *Low-fat*
▽ *Low-calorie*
   Prep time: 10 minutes
   Microwave time: 6 minutes plus
      standing
Ｏ *Degree of difficulty: easy*

2 **tablespoons fresh lemon juice**
1 **tablespoon extra virgin olive oil**
1 **teaspoon drained capers**
½ **teaspoon grated lemon peel**
¼ **teaspoon salt**
¼ **teaspoon freshly ground pepper**
1 **pound sole fillets (about 4 ounces each)**
4 **cups small broccoli florets**

1 Combine the lemon juice, olive oil, capers, lemon peel, salt, and pepper in a small bowl.

2 Arrange the fillets alternately with the broccoli on a 12 or 13-inch microwave-proof plate, leaving the center open. Pour the lemon mixture over fish and broccoli. Cover with plastic wrap, venting on one side to let steam escape. Microwave on high (100% power) for 3 minutes. Rotate the plate and microwave on high (100% power) for 3 minutes more, until fish is just opaque. Cover and let stand 3 minutes before serving. Makes 4 servings.

PER SERVING		DAILY GOAL
Calories	175	2,000 (F), 2,500 (M)
Total fat	5 g	60 g or less (F), 70 g or less (M)
Saturated fat	1 g	20 g or less (F), 23 g or less (M)
Cholesterol	54 mg	300 mg or less
Sodium	278 mg	2,400 mg or less
Carbohydrates	8 g	250 g or more
Protein	26 g	55 g to 90 g

NOTES

68

COD WITH SPICY TOMATO SAUCE

We suggest spinach and rice to round out this flavorful fish dinner. To have everything ready at once, start the rice, then the sauce. And while you microwave the cod, cook the spinach and keep it warm.

Ⓜ   *Microwave*
▼   *Low-fat*
▽   *Low-calorie*
     Prep time: 13 minutes
     Microwave time: 6 to 8 minutes
○   *Degree of difficulty: easy*

3 **teaspoons extra virgin olive oil, divided**
¼ **cup finely chopped onion**
1½ **teaspoons minced garlic, divided**
1 **can (14½ *or* 16 ounces) tomatoes, with their liquid**
½ **teaspoon salt, divided**
⅛ **teaspoon thyme**
5 **tablespoons chopped fresh parsley, divided**
1½ **pounds cod fillets, 1 inch thick**
¼ **teaspoon freshly ground pepper**

1 Heat 1 teaspoon of the oil in a medium skillet over medium heat. Add the onion and cook 3 minutes, until tender. Stir in 1 teaspoon of the garlic and cook 10 seconds. Add the tomatoes with their liquid, ¼ teaspoon of the salt, and thyme. Cook over high heat, breaking up tomatoes with a spoon, about 10 minutes more, until thick. Remove from heat and stir in 2 tablespoons of the parsley. Set the mixture aside.

2 Meanwhile, cut the cod into 4 pieces and arrange it in a shallow microwave-proof dish. Combine the remaining 3 tablespoons parsley, the remaining 2 teaspoons oil, the remaining ½ teaspoon garlic, the remaining ¼ teaspoon salt, and pepper in a small bowl and spread over cod. Cover with wax paper and microwave on high (100% percent) for 6 to 8 minutes, until cod is opaque throughout. Serve with the tomato sauce. Makes 4 servings.

PER SERVING		DAILY GOAL
Calories	255	2,000 (F), 2,500 (M)
Total Fat	6 g	60 g or less (F), 70 g or less (M)
Saturated fat	1 g	20 g or less (F), 23 g or less (M)
Cholesterol	73 mg	300 mg or less
Sodium	526 mg	2,400 mg or less
Carbohydrates	6 g	250 g or more
Protein	32 g	55 g to 90 g

FLOUNDER WITH CILANTRO-CHILE SAUCE

▼ *Low-fat*
▽ *Low-calorie*
Prep time: 15 minutes
Cooking time: 10 minutes
○ *Degree of difficulty: easy*

3 **cups loosely packed fresh cilantro leaves**
⅓ **cup water**
4 **teaspoons fresh lime juice**
4 **fresh Thai red *or* green chiles, seeded and chopped**
¼ **teaspoon salt**
  Pinch granulated sugar
4 **flounder, red snapper, sole, *or* orange roughy fillets (4 ounces each)**

1 Combine the cilantro, water, lime juice, chiles, salt, and sugar in a blender and puree until smooth.

2 Preheat oven to 400°F. Lightly oil 4 squares of foil or parchment paper. Place fish on foil. Sprinkle fish lightly with salt, then spread 2 teaspoons cilantro sauce on each fillet. Fold foil up around fish and crimp edges to seal. Arrange packages on a cookie sheet and bake 10 minutes.

3 Transfer the packages to serving plates and carefully unfold them. Serve fish with additional sauce. Makes 4 servings.

PER SERVING WITH 1 TABLESPOON SAUCE		DAILY GOAL
Calories	135	2,000 (F), 2,500 (M)
Total Fat	3 g	60 g or less (F), 70 g or less (M)
Saturated fat	0 g	20 g or less (F), 23 g or less (M)
Cholesterol	42 mg	300 mg or less
Sodium	348 mg	2,400 mg or less
Carbohydrates	2 g	250 g or more
Protein	24 g	55 g to 90 g

LINGUINE WITH WHITE CLAM SAUCE

▼ *Low-fat*
Prep time: 20 minutes
Cooking time: 30 minutes
○ *Degree of difficulty: easy*

1 **bottle (8 ounces) clam juice**
½ **cup dry white wine**
3 **dozen littleneck clams, scrubbed**
1 **cup finely chopped onions**
1 **cup finely chopped carrots**
½ **cup finely chopped celery**
2 **teaspoons minced garlic**
  Pinch thyme
  Pinch red pepper flakes
2 **tablespoons chopped fresh parsley**
2 **teaspoons extra virgin olive oil**
¼ **teaspoon salt**
1 **pound linguine *or* spaghetti, cooked according to package directions, drained**

1 Bring clam juice and wine to a boil in large pot. Add clams; cover and cook 5 to 6 minutes, until shells open. Transfer clams to a bowl with a slotted spoon; cool. Remove meat from shells and chop coarsely. (Discard any unopened clams.)

2 Add onions, carrots, celery, garlic, thyme, and pepper flakes to clam juice in pot. Simmer over medium heat 25 minutes, until vegetables are tender. Stir in chopped clams, parsley, oil, and salt. Toss sauce with pasta. Makes 6 servings.

PER SERVING		DAILY GOAL
Calories	390	2,000 (F), 2,500 (M)
Total fat	4 g	60 g or less (F), 70 g or less (M)
Saturated fat	1 g	20 g or less (F), 23 g or less (M)
Cholesterol	34 mg	300 mg or less
Sodium	323 mg	2,400 mg or less
Carbohydrates	64 g	250 g or more
Protein	23 g	55 g to 90 g

GOOD FISH SENSE: HOW TO BUY AND STORE FRESH AND FROZEN FISH

Follow your nose

• Fish should always smell clean, not fishy.

• Saltwater fish and shellfish should smell like the sea.

• Shrimp should have a mild natural iodine smell; an ammonia odor indicates deterioration.

• Scallops smell sweet when they're fresh, like sulfur when they aren't.

• Clams, mussels, and oysters smell clean and briny when fresh, strong when they're not.

Take a good look at the fish

• If you are purchasing fish in its whole state, the flesh should spring back when gently pressed and the scales should be tightly attached to the skin and appear shiny. The eyes should be bulging and clear. And don't forget to check the gills—they should appear red or clear pink.

• Fish fillets should be evenly colored with no bruises or browning around the edges. The meat shouldn't be separating much or falling from the bone.

• Clams, oysters, and mussels should be tightly closed and feel heavy for their size. If the shells are open, tap them and they should close immediately. If they don't close they aren't fresh.

• Shucked oysters should be packed in liquid that's clear, not milky.

• Uncooked shrimp are pale pink to shimmery grey and should look firm and plump.

• Fresh scallops should be pinkish, white, or pale yellow and give off a clear liquid. They should also feel firm.

Keep fresh seafood cold

• Place the seafood in a large shallow dish or roasting pan in one layer and cover it with crushed ice, then cover the pan with plastic wrap. Pour off any water and replenish the ice when it's needed. Fresh seafood will only keep up to 2 days in the refrigerator, so it's important to know when it arrived at the market.

• To freeze fish steaks and fillets, wrap them tightly in freezer paper and store up to 3 months at 0°F.

Fresh Seafood vs. Frozen Seafood

• Seafood labeled "fresh" only means that it's never been frozen. but it may have been out of the water for days. Frozen seafood, if it was properly frozen within hours of being removed from the water and kept at steady, cold temperatures, can be better quality than so-called fresh seafood.

• It's best to thaw frozen seafood in the refrigerator, not on the kitchen counter. Or, place frozen seafood in a tightly sealed plastic bag and hold it under cold running water until it has softened.

• Don't cook frozen seafood without thawing it first because it tends to cook unevenly and its texture can be damaged.

BLACKENED SNAPPER WITH CORN RELISH

In this Creole-inspired dish, the fish is rubbed with spices and cooked in a cast iron skillet. The corn-yogurt relish adds a cool note.

▼ *Low-fat*
▽ *Low-calorie*
   Prep time: 15 minutes
   Cooking time: 8 to 10 minutes
      per batch
○ *Degree of difficulty: easy*

1 **cup fresh *or* frozen, thawed corn kernels**
¼ **cup plain low-fat yogurt**
3 **green onions, thinly sliced**
¼ **teaspoon grated lemon peel**
1¼ **teaspoons salt, divided**
¾ **teaspoon freshly ground pepper, divided**
2 **teaspoons paprika**
½ **teaspoon minced garlic**
¼ **teaspoon ground red pepper**
¼ **teaspoon thyme**
¼ **teaspoon oregano**
4 **red snapper fillets (6 ounces each)**

1 Combine the corn, yogurt, onions, lemon peel, ¼ teaspoon of the salt, and ¼ teaspoon of the pepper in a small bowl. Cover and refrigerate until ready to use.

2 Combine the paprika, garlic, the remaining teaspoon salt, the remaining ½ teaspoon pepper, ground red pepper, thyme, and oregano in a pie plate. Dip each fish fillet into the spice mixture to coat both sides.

3 Heat a large cast-iron skillet over high heat until smoking, about 3 minutes. Remove from heat. Coat the skillet with vegetable cooking spray. Add the fish, in batches if necessary, and cook 3 to 5 minutes, until brown and crisp on both sides. Transfer to a serving platter. Serve with corn relish. Makes 4 servings.

PER SERVING		DAILY GOAL
Calories	220	2,000 (F), 2,500 (M)
Total Fat	3 g	60 g or less (F), 70 g or less (M)
Saturated fat	1 g	20 g or less (F), 23 g or less (M)
Cholesterol	64 mg	300 mg or less
Sodium	812 mg	2,400 mg or less
Carbohydrates	10 g	250 g or more
Protein	37 g	55 g to 90 g

73

GULF COAST SEAFOOD GUMBO

All you need is one slice of bacon to capture the smoky flavor typical of this zesty, bayou country fish stew.

▼ *Low-fat*
▽ *Low-calorie*
   Prep time: 20 minutes
   Cooking time: 55 minutes
○ *Degree of difficulty: easy*

1   **slice bacon, chopped**
2   **tablespoons all-purpose flour**
1   **large onion, chopped**
1   **red pepper, cut into ½-inch dice**
1   **green pepper, cut into ½-inch dice**
1   **teaspoon minced garlic**
¾   **teaspoon salt**
¼   **teaspoon freshly ground pepper**
¼   **teaspoon thyme**
⅛ to ¼ **teaspoon ground red pepper**
1   **can (13¾ *or* 14½ ounces) chicken broth, defatted (see tip, page 9)**
1   **cup sliced frozen okra**
1   **cup chopped, drained canned tomatoes**

1   **cup chopped green onions**
1   **pound red snapper *or* catfish fillets, cut into 1½-inch chunks**
8   **ounces medium shrimp, peeled and deveined**
3   **cups cooked long-grain rice**

1 Cook the bacon in a large heavy Dutch oven over medium heat until crisp. Drain on paper towels. Reduce heat to medium-low. Stir the flour into the drippings and cook, stirring frequently, about 12 to 15 minutes, until the mixture is a deep golden brown. (Be careful not to burn.)

2 Stir in the onion, diced red and green peppers, garlic, salt, pepper, thyme, and ground red pepper. Cover and cook, stirring occasionally, 10 minutes, until vegetables are tender.

3 Gradually stir in the broth, okra, tomatoes, and green onions. Return to a simmer and cook, covered, 10 to 15 minutes, until the mixture is thickened and vegetables are tender. Stir in the snapper and shrimp. Cook 5 minutes more or until fish is opaque. Stir in the bacon. Serve over cooked rice. Makes 6 servings.

PER SERVING WITH RICE		DAILY GOAL
Calories	300	2,000 (F), 2,500 (M)
Total Fat	6 g	60 g or less (F), 70 g or less (M)
Saturated fat	1 g	20 g or less (F), 23 g or less (M)
Cholesterol	78 mg	300 mg or less
Sodium	811 mg	2,400 mg or less
Carbohydrates	34 g	250 g or more
Protein	27 g	55 g to 90 g

NOTES

SEAFOOD CHOWDER PROVENÇALE

At the end of a busy week, relax over a bowl of this hearty soup. It has the subtle flavor of fresh fennel, which brings out the natural sweetness of seafood.

▼ *Low-fat*
Prep time: 25 minutes
Cooking time: 50 minutes
○ *Degree of difficulty: easy*

1	tablespoon butter *or* margarine
½	cup finely chopped onion
1	large bulb fennel (anise), cored and sliced thin (2½ cups)
⅛	teaspoon fennel seeds, bruised
2	tablespoons all-purpose flour
½	cup dry white wine
1½	pounds new potatoes, diced
2	cups peeled and diagonally sliced carrots
3	bottles (8 ounces each) clam juice
1	cup water
1	teaspoon salt
¼	teaspoon freshly ground pepper
	Pinch thyme
1	pound cod fillets, cut into chunks
4	ounces shrimp, peeled and deveined
¼	cup chopped fresh parsley
12	slices French bread, toasted
1	large clove garlic, halved

1 Melt the butter in a large pot over medium-low heat. Add the onion, fennel, and fennel seeds. Cook, stirring occasionally, 10 to 15 minutes, until the vegetables are tender. Stir in the flour and cook, stirring, 3 to 4 minutes. Stir in the wine. Bring to a boil and cook 2 minutes more.

2 Add the potatoes, carrots, clam juice, water, salt, pepper, and thyme. Bring to a boil; reduce heat. Cover and simmer 15 minutes, until vegetables are tender. Add the cod and shrimp to pot. Cover and simmer until seafood turns opaque, 4 to 5 minutes.

3 Meanwhile, rub toasted French bread with the cut side of the garlic clove. Ladle the soup into bowls and top with bread. Sprinkle with parsley. Makes 6 servings.

PER SERVING		DAILY GOAL
Calories	380	2,000 (F), 2,500 (M)
Total Fat	4 g	60 g or less (F), 70 g or less (M)
Saturated fat	2 g	20 g or less (F), 23 g or less (M)
Cholesterol	61 mg	300 mg or less
Sodium	1,081 mg	2,400 mg or less
Carbohydrates	55 g	250 g or more
Protein	25 g	55 g to 90 g

NOTES

YUCATECAN GRILLED CATFISH WITH PICKLED RED ONIONS

Catfish, a southern favorite, is now available nationwide at bargain prices. We love this recipe, adapted from Chef Rick Bayless of the Frontera Grill in Chicago. Great for do-ahead entertaining, the catfish is perfect paired with the assertive flavors of the marinade and pickled onions.

▼ *Low-fat*
  Prep time: 20 minutes plus chilling
  Grilling time: 10 minutes
◗ *Degree of difficulty: moderate*

Pickled Red Onions

1	quart water
1½	cups thinly sliced red onion
¼	cup orange juice
¼	cup cider vinegar
4	garlic cloves, peeled and cut in half
2	teaspoons sugar
½	teaspoon cumin
½	teaspoon salt
½	teaspoon freshly ground pepper

Achiote-Marinated Catfish

1½	teaspoons achiote *or* annato seeds*
2½	teaspoons minced garlic
½	teaspoon salt
½	teaspoon cinnamon
½	teaspoon ground coriander
½	teaspoon oregano
½	teaspoon freshly ground pepper
¼	teaspoon cumin
⅛	teaspoon cloves
1½	tablespoons fresh lime juice
4	catfish fillets (1½ pounds)
	Olive oil
2	cups hot cooked rice

1 For Pickled Red Onions, bring water to a boil in a medium saucepan. Add the onions and cook 1 minute. Transfer onions to a large colander and rinse under cold running water; drain. Whisk together the orange juice, vinegar, garlic, sugar, cumin, salt, and pepper in a medium glass bowl to blend. Stir in the onions, cover, and refrigerate 4 hours or overnight.

2 For Achiote-Marinated Catfish, crush achiote seeds against the bottom of a bowl, using a spoon. With the back of a large knife, mash the garlic and salt to form a paste; transfer to a small bowl. Stir in the ground achiote, cinnamon, coriander, oregano, pepper, cumin, cloves, and lime juice until smooth. Spread 2 teaspoons of the marinade on the top and bottom of each catfish fillet. Cover and refrigerate 1 to 2 hours.

3 Prepare the grill; brush the grill rack lightly with the olive oil. Grill the fish over very hot coals 5 minutes per side. Drain Pickled Red Onions and serve with fish and rice. Makes 4 servings.

*Available in Hispanic markets and specialty sections of supermarkets.

PER SERVING		DAILY GOAL
Calories	405	2,000 (F), 2,500 (M)
Total Fat	12 g	60 g or less (F), 70 g or less (M)
Saturated fat	3 g	20 g or less (F), 23 g or less (M)
Cholesterol	56 mg	300 mg or less
Sodium	614 mg	2,400 mg or less
Carbohydrates	41 g	250 g or more
Protein	30 g	55 g to 90 g

NOTES

MARINATED SEAFOOD KEBOBS

The citrus marinade gives scallops and shrimp a taste of the tropics. Serve each portion with a half cup of cooked rice.

▼ *Low-fat*
▽ *Low-calorie*
   Prep time: 15 minutes plus marinating
   Grilling time: 10 minutes
○ *Degree of difficulty: easy*

  2 **tablespoons vegetable oil**
  3 **tablespoons fresh lime juice**
  1 **tablespoon chopped fresh parsley**
  ½ **teaspoon grated lime peel**
  ½ **teaspoon minced garlic**
  ¼ **teaspoon salt**
  ¼ **teaspoon freshly ground pepper**
     Pinch ground red pepper
 12 **ounces sea scallops**
  8 **medium shrimp, shelled and deveined**
 16 **medium fresh mushrooms**
  1 **medium red *or* green pepper, cut into 16 squares**

1 Mix the oil, lime juice, parsley, lime peel, garlic, salt, pepper, and ground red pepper in a shallow bowl. Add the scallops and shrimp, tossing to coat. Marinate at room temperature 25 to 30 minutes. Add the mushrooms and pepper pieces and toss to combine. Marinate 5 minutes more.

2 Meanwhile, prepare the grill or preheat broiler and broiler pan.

3 Thread the scallops, shrimp, mushrooms, and pepper pieces alternately on each of 8 skewers. Reserve marinade. Grill or broil kebobs 4 to 6 inches from heat, brushing several times with marinade and turning occasionally, about 10 minutes, until scallops and shrimp are cooked through and vegetables are tender-crisp. Makes 4 servings.

PER SERVING WITH RICE		DAILY GOAL
Calories	300	2,000 (F), 2,500 (M)
Total Fat	8 g	60 g or less (F), 70 g or less (M)
Saturated fat	1 g	20 g or less (F), 23 g or less (M)
Cholesterol	62 mg	300 mg or less
Sodium	310 mg	2,400 mg or less
Carbohydrates	34 g	250 g or more
Protein	22 g	55 g to 90 g

NOTES

SQUID SALAD WITH BLACK BEANS

This double chile pepper salad from Seppi Renggli, former chef of New York City's famed Four Seasons Restaurant, is perfect warm weather fare. The bean salad can be prepared early in the day, and the squid takes only seconds to cook.

▼ *Low-fat*
▽ *Low-calorie*
  Prep time: 20 minutes plus standing
  Cooking time: 2 to 3 hours
○ *Degree of difficulty: easy*

- 1 **teaspoon cumin seeds**
- 1 **cup dried black beans, rinsed and picked over**
- 1 **small onion, stuck with 4 whole cloves**
- 1 **bay leaf**
- 1 **dried chile pepper**
- 3 **garlic cloves, divided**
- 2 **tablespoons red wine vinegar, divided**
- 2 **tablespoons fresh lemon juice**
- 1 **tablespoon olive oil**
- 2 **shallots, sliced**
- 1 **jalapeño chile, seeded and minced**
- 1 **tablespoon chopped fresh cilantro**
- 10 **ounces cleaned squid, cut into 4-inch pieces**
- 12 **cherry tomatoes, for garnish**
- 4 **lime slices, for garnish**

1 Toast the cumin seeds in a small saucepan over medium heat until fragrant, about 1 minute.

2 Cover the beans with 4 cups cold water in a 2-quart stockpot. Add the onion, bay leaf, chile pepper, 2 cloves of the garlic, and toasted cumin seed; bring to a boil. Cover and simmer about 2 to 3 hours, until beans are soft and all the water is absorbed. Discard onion, bay leaf, chile pepper, and garlic. Toss the hot beans with 1 tablespoon of the vinegar.

3 Slightly crush the remaining 1 clove garlic. Combine the crushed garlic, the remaining 1 tablespoon vinegar, lemon juice, olive oil, shallots, jalapeño, and cilantro in a small bowl. Whisk well and let stand at least 30 minutes.

4 Bring a large saucepan of water to a boil. Lightly score the underside of each piece of squid and blanch 5 seconds. Drain and plunge the squid immediately into a bowl of ice water. Drain squid again and pat dry on paper towels. Cut the squid into narrow strips and transfer it to a large bowl.

5 Discard garlic from dressing; whisk well, and toss with squid. Divide squid among 4 serving plates and surround with beans. Garnish with cherry tomatoes and lime slices, if desired. Makes 4 servings.

PER SERVING		DAILY GOAL
Calories	280	2,000 (F), 2,500 (M)
Total fat	5 g	60 g or less (F), 70 g or less (M)
Saturated fat	1 g	20 g or less (F), 23 g or less (M)
Cholesterol	165 mg	300 mg or less
Sodium	38 mg	2,400 mg or less
Carbohydrates	36 g	250 g or more
Protein	22 g	55 g to 90 g

NOTES

GRILLED SHRIMP WITH HERBS AND WHITE WINE

We received this speedy marinated shrimp from Julie Williams, co-owner of the Frog's Leap Winery in California's Napa Valley. Serve it with rice and grilled tomato halves and be sure to provide plenty of napkins because your guests peel the shrimp themselves.

▼ *Low-fat*
▽ *Low-calorie*
  Prep time: 10 minutes plus marinating
  Grilling time: 3 to 6 minutes
○ *Degree of difficulty: easy*

1½ **pounds medium shrimp, unpeeled**
 ½ **cup minced fresh dill *or* basil**
 1 **tablespoon extra virgin olive oil**
 1 **tablespoon minced garlic**
 1 **teaspoon salt**
 1 **teaspoon red pepper flakes**
 ¼ **cup dry white wine**

1 Rinse the shrimp. Combine the shrimp, dill, oil, garlic, salt, and red pepper in a large bowl. Cover and refrigerate 30 to 60 minutes.

2 Prepare the grill or preheat broiler. Ten minutes before cooking, add the wine to the shrimp and toss. With a slotted spoon, arrange shrimp on the grill or broiler pan. Cook 1½ to 3 minutes per side, just until opaque throughout. Serve immediately. Makes 4 servings.

PER SERVING		DAILY GOAL
Calories	170	2,000 (F), 2,500 (M)
Total Fat	4 g	60 g or less (F), 70 g or less (M)
Saturated fat	1 g	20 g or less (F), 23 g or less (M)
Cholesterol	210 mg	300 mg or less
Sodium	482 mg	2,400 mg or less
Carbohydrates	3 g	250 g or more
Protein	28 g	55 g to 90 g

NOTES

80

SHRIMP WITH FETA AND DILL

Here's a lovely rice pilaf that boasts an unusual combination of seafood and cheese. Remember that some varieties of feta are very salty. Start with ¼ teaspoon of salt, and add more as needed.

▼ *Low-fat*
▽ *Low-calorie*
   Prep time: 40 minutes
   Cooking time: 7 minutes
○ *Degree of difficulty: easy*

¾ cup long-grain rice
1 pint cherry tomatoes, quartered
1 package (10 ounces) frozen
      chopped spinach, thawed and
      squeezed dry
2 tablespoons chopped fresh dill
1 teaspoon minced garlic
¼ to ½ teaspoon salt
¼ teaspoon freshly ground pepper
1 teaspoon extra virgin olive oil
1 pound medium shrimp, peeled and
      deveined
⅓ cup crumbled feta cheese
1 tablespoon freshly grated Parmesan
      cheese

1 Cook the rice according to package directions. Transfer the rice to a medium bowl. Stir in the tomatoes, spinach, dill, garlic, salt, and pepper.

2 Heat the oil in a large nonstick skillet over medium-high heat. Add the shrimp and cook, stirring, 3 to 4 minutes, until opaque. Set aside and keep warm. Add the rice mixture to skillet and cook, stirring, 2 to 3 minutes, until heated through and tomatoes begin to wilt. Remove from heat and stir in the feta.

3 Transfer the rice mixture to a serving platter and top with shrimp. Sprinkle with Parmesan. Makes 4 servings.

PER SERVING		DAILY GOAL	
Calories	300	2,000 (F), 2,500 (M)	
Total Fat	6 g	60 g or less (F), 70 g or less (M)	
Saturated fat	2 g	20 g or less (F), 23 g or less (M)	
Cholesterol	151 mg	300 mg or less	
Sodium	617 mg	2,400 mg or less	
Carbohydrates	35 g	250 g or more	
Protein	26 g	55 g to 90 g	

81

SHRIMP-COUSCOUS SALAD WITH CARROT-GINGER VINAIGRETTE

This unusual seafood salad can be prepared with carrot juice you juice at home or purchased carrot juice, available in most health food stores.

▼ *Low-fat*
▽ *Low-calorie*
  Prep time: 20 minutes plus cooling
  Cooking time: 10 minutes
○ *Degree of difficulty: easy*

Couscous
2¼ **cups fresh carrot juice**
½ **stick cinnamon**
½ **teaspoon salt**
1 **box (10 ounces) quick-cooking couscous (1⅓ cups)**
½ **cup frozen peas, thawed**
½ **cup finely diced jicama**
3 **green onions, thinly sliced**

Carrot-Ginger Vinaigrette
½ **cup fresh carrot juice**
3 **tablespoons olive oil**
1 **teaspoon grated fresh ginger**
  Salt
  Freshly ground pepper
8 **cups assorted baby lettuces**

1 **pound shrimp, cooked and peeled and deveined**
  Lemon wedges

1 For Couscous, bring the carrot juice to a boil in a medium saucepan with cinnamon stick and salt. Stir in the couscous. Remove from heat, cover, and let stand 5 minutes. Fluff couscous with a fork. Transfer the couscous to a large bowl and cool to room temperature. Stir in the peas, jicama, and green onions.

2 For the Carrot-Ginger Vinaigrette, bring the carrot juice to a boil in a small saucepan and boil until reduced to ¼ cup. Transfer the juice to a medium bowl and cool to room temperature. Whisk in the oil, ginger, salt, and pepper to taste.

3 Toss the lettuces with 2 tablespoons of the vinaigrette in a large bowl. Arrange lettuce on a large platter or 6 dinner plates.

Toss the shrimp in a small bowl with another 2 tablespoons of the vinaigrette. Add the remaining vinaigrette to couscous and toss with a fork to combine.

4 Spoon couscous on top of greens and top with shrimp. Serve with lemon wedges. Makes 6 servings.

PER SERVING		DAILY GOAL
Calories	375	2,000 (F), 2,500 (M)
Total Fat	6 g	60 g or less (F), 70 g or less (M)
Saturated fat	1 g	20 g or less (F), 23 g or less (M)
Cholesterol	93 mg	300 mg or less
Sodium	330 mg	2,400 mg or less
Carbohydrates	53 g	250 g or more
Protein	21 g	55 g to 90 g

NOTES

83

SHRIMP SCAMPI WITH SPINACH

This perfect marriage of flavors tastes like scampi, but without the fattening butter. Crusty bread is a must for soaking up all the scrumptious juices. Microwaving the shrimp on medium prevents them from cooking too quickly and getting tough.

Ⓜ   *Microwave*
▼   *Low-fat*
▽   *Low-calorie*
    Prep time: 15 minutes plus standing
    Microwave time: 10 to 16 minutes
O   *Degree of difficulty: easy*

¼   **cup chopped fresh parsley**
1   **tablespoon minced shallots**
2   **teaspoons minced garlic**
1   **teaspoon olive oil**
½   **teaspoon salt**
¼   **teaspoon freshly ground pepper**
¼   **teaspoon grated lemon peel**
1¼ **pounds medium shrimp, peeled and deveined**
1   **pound fresh spinach, rinsed and stems removed**
    Lemon wedges, for garnish

1 Combine the parsley, shallots, garlic, oil, salt, pepper, and lemon peel in a 9-inch microwave-proof pie plate. Add the shrimp and toss to coat evenly. Refrigerate 15 minutes.

2 Meanwhile, place the spinach with water clinging to its leaves in a 2-quart microwave-proof casserole. Cover and microwave on high (100% power) for 5 to 8 minutes, stirring once after 3 minutes. Let stand.

3 Cover the shrimp and microwave on medium (50% power) for 5 to 8 minutes, until just pink. Let stand 2 minutes.

4 Drain the spinach and place on a serving platter, then top with the shrimp mixture. Garnish platter with lemon wedges, if desired. Serve with steamed rice and crusty bread. Makes 4 servings.

PER SERVING		DAILY GOAL
Calories	180	2,000 (F), 2,500 (M)
Total fat	4 g	60 g or less (F), 70 g or less (M)
Saturated fat	1 g	20 g or less (F), 23 g or less (M)
Cholesterol	209 mg	300 mg or less
Sodium	543 mg	2,400 mg or less
Carbohydrates	5 g	250 g or more
Protein	30 g	55 g to 90 g

NOTES

84

MARINATED SHRIMP WITH MANGO RELISH

This recipe, adapted from the original by Chris Schlesinger and John Willoughby, is a refreshing fruit salsa served along seasoned grilled shrimp.

▼ *Low-fat*
▽ *Low-calorie*
   Prep time: 40 minutes plus marinating
   Grilling time: 2 to 6 minutes
O *Degree of difficulty: easy*

1½ cups pineapple juice
½ cup dark rum
¼ cup fresh lime juice
2 tablespoons chopped fresh cilantro
1 teaspoon minced garlic
1 teaspoon salt
½ teaspoon cracked black pepper
2 pounds medium shrimp, unpeeled

Mango Relish
2 mangos, finely diced
½ cup finely diced red pepper
½ cup finely diced green pepper
⅓ cup finely chopped red onion
2 tablespoons fresh lime juice

1 tablespoon red wine vinegar
½ teaspoon minced garlic
15 whole cilantro leaves
¼ teaspoon salt
¼ teaspoon freshly ground pepper

1 Combine the pineapple juice, rum, lime juice, chopped cilantro, garlic, salt, and pepper in a large bowl. Add the shrimp, cover, and refrigerate 2 to 4 hours.

2 For Mango Relish, combine mangos, red and green peppers, red onion, lime juice, vinegar, garlic, cilantro leaves, salt, and pepper in a medium bowl. (Can be made ahead. Cover and refrigerate up to 4 hours.)

3 Prepare the grill. Thread the shrimp on skewers. Grill shrimp over medium-hot coals 1 to 3 minutes per side, until opaque. Spread the Mango Relish on a platter and arrange the shrimp on top. Makes 6 servings.

PER SERVING		DAILY GOAL
Calories	225	2,000 (F), 2,500 (M)
Total fat	2 g	60 g or less (F), 70 g or less (M)
Saturated fat	0 g	20 g or less (F), 23 g or less (M)
Cholesterol	186 mg	300 mg or less
Sodium	458 mg	2,400 mg or less
Carbohydrates	20 g	250 g or more
Protein	26 g	55 g to 90 g

CLASSICS WITH

A LIGHT TOUCH

With just the right amount of trimming, we've lightened some of your favorite main dishes. And, we've kept each new dish just as luscious as the original. You won't feel guilty taking the plunge with great tasting choices such as Fettuccine Bolognese and Creole Pepper Steaks. Or, warm up with Winter's Eve Borscht or Spiced Shepherd's Pie with mashed potatoes. Can foods this delectable be good for you? They can now!

CREOLE PEPPER STEAK WITH GRITS

Lean meat tends to stick in nonstick pans so we've come up with a sure-fire solution. Pat the meat with a paper towel before browning it to remove surface moisture.

▼ *Low-fat*
  Prep time: 15 minutes
  Cooking time: 1 hour
○ *Degree of difficulty: easy*

12 ounces beef round steak
¾ teaspoon salt
3 teaspoons vegetable oil, divided
1 cup finely chopped onions
½ cup finely chopped celery
1 red pepper, diced
2 tablespoons all-purpose flour
2 teaspoons minced garlic
¼ teaspoon ground red pepper
1 can (14 *or* 16 ounces) plum
    tomatoes, with their liquid
½ cup chicken broth, defatted
    (see tip, page 9)
¼ teaspoon thyme
½ teaspoon freshly ground pepper

1 tablespoon chopped fresh parsley
1 cup grits, cooked according to
    package directions

1 Slice the steak diagonally across the grain into ¼-inch-thick strips then cut the strips into squares. Pat meat dry with paper towels. Sprinkle with salt.

2 Heat 1 teaspoon of the oil in a large nonstick skillet over medium-high heat. Add a third of the meat and cook until well browned on both sides. Transfer the meat to a plate with a slotted spoon and set aside. Repeat in 2 more batches with the remaining oil and meat.

3 Reduce heat to medium. Add the onions, celery, and diced pepper to skillet. Cook, stirring occasionally, about 5 minutes, until softened. Stir in the flour, garlic, and ground red pepper and cook 1 minute. Add the tomatoes with their liquid, chicken broth, thyme, and pepper. Bring to a boil, stirring and breaking up tomatoes with a spoon. Return meat to skillet. Reduce heat and simmer covered 1 hour. Sprinkle with parsley and serve with grits. Makes 4 servings.

PER SERVING		DAILY GOAL
Calories	410	2,000 (F), 2,500 (M)
Total Fat	15 g	60 g or less (F), 70 g or less (M)
Saturated fat	5 g	20 g or less (F), 23 g or less (M)
Cholesterol	53 mg	300 mg or less
Sodium	779 mg	2,400 mg or less
Carbohydrates	44 g	250 g or more
Protein	23 g	55 g to 90 g

NOTES

PORK CHOP HARVEST

Simmered apples and sweet potatoes with a touch of cinnamon and clove give this cozy main dish a rich taste without the fat or calories.

▼   *Low-fat*
▽   *Low-calorie*
    Prep time: 15 minutes
    Cooking time: 40 minutes
○   *Degree of difficulty: easy*

4   **lean pork loin chops (4 ounces each with bone), trimmed**
1   **garlic clove, halved**
    Salt
    Freshly ground pepper
¼   **teaspoon cinnamon**
1   **cup apple cider *or* juice**
1   **large sweet potato (12 ounces), peeled and sliced**
1   **whole clove**
2   **apples, cored and sliced**
1   **tablespoon cornstarch**
¼   **cup water**
1   **tablespoon cider vinegar**

1 Rub both sides of the pork chops with the garlic and sprinkle with salt and pepper. Spray a large skillet with vegetable cooking spray and heat over medium-high heat. Add chops and brown on both sides.

2 Meanwhile, blend ½ teaspoon salt, cinnamon, and cider in a small bowl. Add the cider mixture, sweet potatoes, and clove to skillet. Reduce heat, cover, and simmer 30 minutes.

3 Uncover skillet and add the apples; simmer 5 minutes more. With a slotted spoon, transfer the pork, potatoes, and apples to a warm platter and keep warm.

4 For sauce, blend the cornstarch with the water in a small bowl. Stir in the vinegar. Add the cornstarch mixture to skillet and simmer, stirring, 5 minutes, until thickened. Serve sauce with pork, sweet potatoes, and apples. Makes 4 servings.

PER SERVING		DAILY GOAL	
Calories	250	2,000 (F), 2,500 (M)	
Total Fat	4 g	60 g or less (F), 70 g or less (M)	
Saturated fat	1 g	20 g or less (F), 23 g or less (M)	
Cholesterol	46 mg	300 mg or less	
Sodium	332 mg	2,400 mg or less	
Carbohydrates	35 g	250 g or more	
Protein	17 g	55 g to 90 g	

89

SPICED SHEPHERD'S PIE

Here's a version of shepherd's pie from cookbook author Beatrice Ojakangas that features flavors from the Adriatic. The crown of mashed potatoes is flavored with feta cheese, and the meat is redolent with aromatic cinnamon and allspice. *Also pictured on page 86.*

▼ *Low-fat*
▽ *Low-calorie*
  Prep time: 40 minutes
  Cooking time: 35 to 40 minutes
◕ *Degree of difficulty: moderate*

  2 **teaspoons olive oil**
  1 **cup chopped onions**
  1 **teaspoon minced garlic**
  2 **pounds lean (90%) ground beef**
  1 **can (14½ *or* 16 ounces) whole tomatoes, with their liquid**
  2 **teaspoons dry mint**
1¾ **teaspoons salt, divided**
  1 **teaspoon cinnamon**
  ½ **teaspoon allspice**
  ¼ **teaspoon freshly ground pepper**
  3 **pounds all-purpose potatoes, peeled and cut into 2-inch pieces**
     Water
  1 **tablespoon butter *or* margarine**
  ¼ **teaspoon freshly ground pepper**
  ½ **cup crumbled feta cheese**

1 Heat the oil in a large skillet over medium-high heat. Add the onions and garlic and cook 1 minute until softened. Add the beef, stirring to break up meat with a spoon, and cook 5 to 7 minutes, until no longer pink. Drain the tomatoes, reserving ⅓ cup of their liquid. Add the drained tomatoes and reserved liquid to skillet with the mint, 1¼ teaspoons of the salt, cinnamon, allspice, and pepper. Cook 3 minutes, breaking up tomatoes with back of a spoon. Transfer the meat mixture to a shallow 2-quart casserole.

2 Meanwhile, preheat oven to 400°F. Combine the potatoes, the remaining ½ teaspoon salt, and enough water to cover in a large saucepan; bring to a boil. Reduce heat and simmer 15 to 20 minutes, until tender. Drain potatoes in a large colander, reserving ½ cup cooking liquid.

3 Transfer the potatoes to a large bowl. With a potato masher, mash the potatoes with the butter. Stir in the reserved potato water, pepper, and cheese. Spoon the potato mixture over the beef filling, mounding it with back of a spoon. Bake 35 to 40 minutes, until top is lightly browned. Makes 8 servings.

PER SERVING		DAILY GOAL
Calories	360	2,000 (F), 2,500 (M)
Total Fat	16 g	60 g or less (F), 70 g or less (M)
Saturated fat	7 g	20 g or less (F), 23 g or less (M)
Cholesterol	82 mg	300 mg or less
Sodium	769 mg	2,400 mg or less
Carbohydrates	28 g	250 g or more
Protein	27 g	55 g to 90 g

NOTES

PORK AND WHITE-BEAN CASSOULET

Long, slow cooking is the key to the good flavor of this classic French bean stew with lean sausage and pork.

▼ *Low-fat*
▽ *Low-calorie*
Prep time: 20 minutes plus soaking
Cooking time: 2 hours
○ *Degree of difficulty: easy*

1 **pound dried Great Northern beans**
1 **teaspoon vegetable oil, divided**
1 **pound boneless pork shoulder,
cut into ¾-inch cubes**
1 **teaspoon salt**
1½ **teaspoons freshly ground pepper,
divided**
2 **cups chopped onions**
1 **tablespoon minced garlic**
8 **ounces light kielbasa, halved
lengthwise and sliced into
½-inch pieces**

2 **cans (13¾ or 14½ ounces each)
chicken broth, defatted (see tip,
page 9) plus enough water to
equal 4½ cups**
½ **bay leaf**
½ **teaspoon thyme**
½ **cup white wine**
2 **tablespoons tomato paste**
1 **pound rutabaga (yellow turnip),
cut into ½-inch dice**
2 **cups peeled sliced carrots**
¼ **cup chopped fresh parsley**

1 Rinse the beans and pick over for small stones and shriveled beans. In a large bowl, cover beans with 2 inches water and soak overnight. (To quick-soak: Combine beans and water to cover 2 inches in a large saucepan and bring to a boil; boil 2 minutes. Cover and let stand 1 hour.) Drain in a colander; set aside.

2 Preheat oven to 350°F. Heat ½ teaspoon of the oil in a large Dutch oven over high heat. Sprinkle half the pork with ½ teaspoon of the salt and pepper; add to Dutch oven and brown well on all sides, 5 minutes. Transfer the pork to a bowl with a slotted spoon. Repeat process with remaining oil, pork, salt, and ½ teaspoon pepper.

3 Reduce heat to medium. Add the onions to Dutch oven and cook, stirring occasionally 5 minutes, until tender. Stir in the garlic and cook until fragrant, 30 seconds. Return pork to pot and add the beans, sausage, broth and water, bay leaf, thyme, and the remaining ½ teaspoon pepper. Bring to a boil. Cover and transfer to the oven.

4 Bake 1 hour. Combine the wine and tomato paste in a small bowl and stir into the pot with the rutabaga and carrots. Cover and bake 1 hour more. (Can be made ahead. Cover and refrigerate 24 hours. Stir in an additional 1 cup water if mixture seems dry. Reheat in oven at 350°F. 1 hour.) Sprinkle with parsley. Makes 12 cups.

PER SERVING		DAILY GOAL
Calories	315	2,000 (F), 2,500 (M)
Total Fat	12 g	60 g or less (F), 70 g or less (M)
Saturated fat	2 g	20 g or less (F), 23 g or less (M)
Cholesterol	40 mg	300 mg or less
Sodium	745 mg	2,400 mg or less
Carbohydrates	32 g	250 g or more
Protein	19 g	55 g to 90 g

BLACK-BEAN AND SMOKY-HAM SOUP

Smoked ham hocks provide the flavor in this classic bean soup. Sliced lemon is the classic garnish, but you can also try chopped red onion and yogurt.

▼   *Low-fat*
▽   *Low-calorie*
   Prep time: 45 minutes plus soaking
   Cooking time: 1½ to 2 hours
○   *Degree of difficulty: easy*

1   **pound dried black beans**
1   **tablespoon vegetable oil**
2   **cups chopped onions**
1   **cup peeled chopped carrots**
1   **cup chopped celery**
1   **tablespoon minced garlic**
2   **teaspoons cumin**
¼   **to ½ teaspoon red pepper flakes**
2   **cans (13¾ or 14½ ounces each) chicken broth, defatted (see tip, page 9)**
4   **cups water**
½   **bay leaf**
¼   **teaspoon thyme**
1   **pound smoked ham hocks**
1   **can (14½ or 16 ounces) tomatoes, chopped with their liquid**
1½   **teaspoons salt**
   Lemon slices, for garnish

1   Rinse the beans and pick over for small stones and shriveled beans. In a large bowl, cover beans with 2 inches water and soak overnight. (To quick-soak: Combine beans with water to cover 2 inches in a large saucepan and bring to a boil; boil 2 minutes. Cover and let stand 1 hour.) Drain in a colander; set aside.

2   Heat the oil in a large Dutch oven over medium heat. Add the onions, carrots, and celery. Cook, stirring occasionally, 10 minutes, until tender. Add the garlic, cumin, and pepper flakes and cook 30 seconds. Stir in the beans, broth, water, bay leaf, thyme, and ham hocks; bring to a boil. Reduce heat, cover, and simmer 30 minutes. Stir in the tomatoes and their liquid and the salt. Cover and simmer 1 to 1½ hours more, until beans are very tender.

3   Remove ham hocks. When cool enough to handle, cut the meat from the bone and dice. Discard skin and bone and bay leaf and return the meat to the soup.

With a potato masher, mash soup to thicken. Spoon into soup bowls and garnish each with a lemon slice, if desired. Makes 12 cups.

PER 1 CUP SERVING		DAILY GOAL
Calories	195	2,000 (F), 2,500 (M)
Total Fat	4 g	60 g or less (F), 70 g or less (M)
Saturated fat	1 g	20 g or less (F), 23 g or less (M)
Cholesterol	7 mg	300 mg or less
Sodium	853 mg	2,400 mg or less
Carbohydrates	30 g	250 g or more
Protein	12 g	55 g to 90 g

NOTES

93

WINTER'S EVE BORSCHT

We've trimmed the fat but doubled the veggies in this classic Eastern European beet soup. This dish takes some time to simmer, but refrigerates beautifully if you want to make it ahead and reheat it later.

▼ *Low-fat*
▽ *Low-calorie*
   Prep time: 35 minutes
   Cooking time: 2 hours 20 minutes
○ *Degree of difficulty: easy*

1	pound lean boneless beef chuck, cut into small chunks
	Salt
	Freshly ground pepper
1	pound diced carrots
3	cups diced onions
2	cans (13¾ *or* 14½ ounces each) beef broth, defatted (see tip, page 9)
4	cups water, divided
1	bay leaf
2	whole cloves
1	pound fresh beets, peeled and julienned
1	pound all-purpose potatoes, peeled and diced
1	pound celery root, peeled and diced
4	cups diced red cabbage
¼	cup red wine vinegar
¼	cup chopped fresh dill
½	cup plain low-fat yogurt

1 Spray a heavy Dutch oven with vegetable cooking spray and heat over medium-high heat. Pat the meat dry with paper towels and sprinkle it lightly with salt and pepper. Add meat to Dutch oven and cook until well browned on all sides. Reduce heat to medium. Stir in the carrots and onions and cook about 7 minutes, until vegetables are tender. Add the beef broth, 2 cups of the water, bay leaf, and cloves; bring to a simmer. Cover Dutch oven tightly with foil and top with a lid. Simmer over low heat 1½ hours, until meat is very tender.

2 Discard the foil and stir in the remaining 2 cups water, beets, potatoes, celery root, and cabbage. Cover and simmer over medium heat 45 minutes, until vegetables are tender. Season with vinegar, dill, 1½ teaspoons salt, and ½ teaspoon pepper. Simmer, uncovered, 5 minutes more. Remove bay leaf. (Can be made ahead. Cool and transfer to a freezer-proof container. Cover and freeze up to 1 month.) Serve with yogurt. Makes 12 cups.

PER CUP WITH YOGURT		DAILY GOAL
Calories	155	2,000 (F), 2,500 (M)
Total Fat	3 g	60 g or less (F), 70 g or less (M)
Saturated fat	1 g	20 g or less (F), 23 g or less (M)
Cholesterol	25 mg	300 mg or less
Sodium	689 mg	2,400 mg or less
Carbohydrates	21 g	250 g or more
Protein	11 g	55 g to 90 g

NOTES

_____

_____

_____

_____

_____

_____

ASIAN STIR-FRY NOODLES WITH BOK CHOY

Bok choy is a variety of Chinese cabbage with long white stalks and wide dark green leaves. Crunchy and mild tasting, it's the perfect texture for stir-frying.

▼ *Low-fat*
▽ *Low-calorie*
Prep time: 20 minutes
Cooking time: 5 minutes
○ *Degree of difficulty: easy*

4 **tablespoons reduced-sodium soy sauce, divided**
2 **teaspoons minced garlic, divided**
1½ **cups cubed firm tofu (8 ounces)**
1 **tablespoon vegetable oil**
1 **teaspoon grated fresh ginger**
4 **cups shredded bok choy**
1 **cup sliced fresh mushrooms**
4 **ounces baked sliced ham, julienned**
8 **ounces Japanese somen noodles *or* vermicelli, cooked according to package directions, drained**

2 **tablespoons chicken broth, defatted (see tip, page 9)**
   Salt
   Freshly ground pepper

1 Combine 2 tablespoons of the soy sauce and 1 teaspoon of the garlic in a medium bowl. Add the tofu and toss to coat.

2 Heat the oil in a wok or large skillet over medium-high heat. Add the remaining 1 teaspoon garlic and ginger and cook until fragrant, 30 seconds. Add the bok choy and mushrooms and stir-fry 2 to 3 minutes, until vegetables are tender-crisp. Gently stir in the tofu mixture and ham and heat through.

3 Stir in the cooked noodles, the remaining 2 tablespoons soy sauce, chicken broth, and salt and pepper to taste, tossing gently until well combined. Makes 6 servings.

PER SERVING		DAILY GOAL
Calories	235	2,000 (F), 2,500 (M)
Total Fat	6 g	60 g or less (F), 70 g or less (M)
Saturated fat	1 g	20 g or less (F), 23 g or less (M)
Cholesterol	11 mg	300 mg or less
Sodium	1,437 mg	2,400 mg or less
Carbohydrates	32 g	250 g or more
Protein	13 g	55 g to 90 g

NOTES

ROSEMARY PORK ROAST WITH COGNAC GLAZE

It is perfectly safe to eat lean cuts of pork that have been roasted to 155°F. For accurate temperature readings, we suggest investing in a good meat thermometer.

▼ *Low-fat*
▽ *Low-calorie*
   Prep time: 10 minutes plus marinating
   Cooking time: 1 hour 10 minutes
○ *Degree of difficulty: easy*

¾ **teaspoon rosemary**
2 **pounds boneless pork loin roast**
1 **tablespoon honey**
1 **tablespoon cognac *or* brandy**
1 **teaspoon salt, divided**
½ **cup water**
1 **tablespoon cornstarch**
1 **cup beef broth, defatted**
   (see tip, page 9)

1 Rub the rosemary over the pork roast. Cover the roast with plastic wrap and refrigerate 8 hours or overnight.

2 Preheat oven to 325°F. Combine the honey and cognac in a small bowl. Sprinkle ½ teaspoon of the salt over pork and place on a rack in a roasting pan. Roast, basting frequently, 1 hour, until meat thermometer reaches 155°F. Transfer the meat to a platter and let stand 10 minutes.

3 Meanwhile, stir together the water and cornstarch in a small bowl. Heat the drippings in the roasting pan over high heat. Add the beef broth, stirring to scrape up browned bits. Bring to a boil. Whisk in the dissolved water-cornstarch mixture and add the remaining ½ teaspoon salt. Return to boil; boil 1 minute. Slice the pork thinly and serve with sauce. Makes 8 servings.

PER SERVING		DAILY GOAL
Calories	180	2,000 (F), 2,500 (M)
Total Fat	6 g	60 g or less (F), 70 g or less (M)
Saturated fat	2 g	20 g or less (F), 23 g or less (M)
Cholesterol	71 mg	300 mg or less
Sodium	481 mg	2,400 mg or less
Carbohydrates	3 g	250 g or more
Protein	25 g	55 g to 90 g

GOOD FORTUNE HOPPIN' JOHN WITH HAM AND GREENS

In the South on New Year's Day, black-eyed peas and greens are served as symbols of good luck and wealth. It's your good fortune that our version is lower in fat, so your resolution to eat more healthfully in the New Year will be a lot easier to keep.

▼ *Low-fat*
▽ *Low-calorie*
   Prep time: 10 minutes
   Cooking time: 1 hour
○ *Degree of difficulty: easy*

  3 **cups water**
  1 **cup dried black-eyed peas**
  ½ **cup finely chopped onion**
  ½ **cup finely chopped carrots**
  ½ **cup finely chopped celery**
  1 **slice bacon, diced**
  ½ **teaspoon red pepper flakes**
  1 **teaspoon salt, divided**
  ½ **cup long-grain rice**

  ½ **cup chicken broth, defatted
     (see tip, page 9)**
1½ **pounds mixed collard, mustard
     greens, kale, *or* spinach,
     chopped**
  1 **ham steak (¾ to 1 pound), broiled
     Hot pepper sauce**

1 Combine the water, black-eyed peas, onion, carrots, celery, bacon, and red pepper flakes in a large saucepan. Bring to a boil; cover and simmer 30 minutes. Stir in ½ teaspoon of the salt and simmer covered 30 minutes more, until tender.

2 Meanwhile, cook the rice according to package directions. Stir rice into black-eyed pea mixture.

3 Bring the chicken broth to a boil in a large saucepan. Add the greens and the remaining ½ teaspoon salt. Cook, stirring occasionally, 15 minutes, until tender. (If using only spinach, reduce broth to ¼ cup and cook spinach 5 minutes.) Serve with black-eyed peas (Hoppin' John), ham, and hot pepper sauce. Makes 4 servings.

PER SERVING		DAILY GOAL
Calories	475	2,000 (F), 2,500 (M)
Total Fat	10 g	60 g or less (F), 70 g or less (M)
Saturated fat	3 g	20 g or less (F), 23 g or less (M)
Cholesterol	51 mg	300 mg or less
Sodium	2,238 mg	2,400 mg or less
Carbohydrates	63 g	250 g or more
Protein	36 g	55 g to 90 g

NOTES

GINGER-GLAZED BAKED HAM

If you can't find ginger conserve in your local gourmet store, use a combination of marmalade and chopped crystallized ginger.

▼　Low-fat
▽　Low-calorie
　　Prep time: 5 minutes
　　Cooking time: 1¼ hours
○　*Degree of difficulty: easy*

1　**bone-in smoked half ham (7 pounds)**
2　**cups water**
½　**cup ginger conserve** *or* **⅓ cup orange marmalade plus 2 tablespoons minced crystallized ginger**
¼　**cup firmly packed brown sugar**
1　**teaspoon dry mustard**
2　**tablespoons dry sherry**

1 Preheat oven to 325°F. Lightly score the top of the ham with a sharp knife. Place in a shallow roasting pan with water. Bake 1¼ hours, basting every 20 minutes.

2 Meanwhile, combine the ginger conserve, sugar, mustard, and sherry in a medium bowl.

3 During the last 20 minutes of baking, spread the top of the ham with glaze. Transfer the meat to a serving platter and cut into thin slices. Makes 12 servings.

PER 3-OUNCE SERVING		DAILY GOAL
Calories	140	2,000 (F), 2,500 (M)
Total Fat	4 g	60 g or less (F), 70 g or less (M)
Saturated fat	1 g	20 g or less (F), 23 g or less (M)
Cholesterol	40 mg	300 mg or less
Sodium	1,216 mg	2,400 mg or less
Carbohydrates	7 g	250 g or more
Protein	16 g	55 g to 90 g

PORK FAJITAS

This lean fajita filling with red and green peppers is ready in a flash. You can choose to indulge by adding flavorful garnishes such as shredded lettuce, chopped avocado, cilantro, tomatoes, or chopped olives.

▼ *Low-fat*
▽ *Low-calorie*
  Prep time: 20 minutes
  Cooking time: 7 minutes
○ *Degree of difficulty: easy*

  1 **teaspoon olive oil**
  1 **pound pork tenderloin, julienned**
  ½ **teaspoon salt**
  ¼ **teaspoon freshly ground pepper**
  1 **red pepper, julienned**
  1 **green pepper, julienned**
  1 **small onion, thinly sliced**
  1 **garlic clove, minced**
  ½ **teaspoon cumin**
  2 **teaspoons fresh lime juice**
  8 **flour tortillas (6-inch), warmed**

  ½ **cup prepared salsa**
     Shredded lettuce, chopped
       avocado, cilantro, tomatoes
       and/or **olives, for garnish**
       (optional)

1 Heat the oil in a large skillet over high heat. Add the pork and sprinkle with the salt and pepper. Cook and stir, 2 minutes. Stir in the red and green peppers, onion, garlic, and cumin. Cook 3 to 4 minutes more, until vegetables are tender-crisp. Stir in the lime juice.

2 To serve, roll ¾ cup pork mixture in each warm tortilla. Top with 1 tablespoon salsa and your choice of garnishes, if desired. Makes 4 servings.

PER SERVING WITHOUT GARNISHES		DAILY GOAL
Calories	325	2,000 (F), 2,500 (M)
Total Fat	10 g	60 g or less (F), 70 g or less (M)
Saturated fat	3 g	20 g or less (F), 23 g or less (M)
Cholesterol	75 mg	300 mg or less
Sodium	702 mg	2,400 mg or less
Carbohydrates	30 g	250 g or more
Protein	28 g	55 g to 90 g

NOTES

HERB-ROASTED PORK WITH APPLES

Since pork tenderloin is usually sold two per package, it's always great to have an extra one in the freezer for later use. Thaw in the refrigerator overnight.

▼   *Low-fat*
▽   *Low-calorie*
     Prep time: 15 minutes plus marinating
     Cooking time: 25 minutes
○   *Degree of difficulty: easy*

  1   **teaspoon minced garlic**
  ½   **teaspoon rosemary, crumbled**
  ½   **teaspoon freshly ground pepper**
  ¼   **teaspoon thyme, crumbled**
  ¼   **teaspoon salt**
  1   **pork tenderloin (12 to 14 ounces)**
  ⅓   **cup minced shallots**
  3   **Granny Smith apples, sliced**
  2   **tablespoons granulated sugar**
  1   **cup chicken broth, defatted**
       (see tip, page 9)
  ½   **cup dry white wine**

1 Combine the garlic, rosemary, pepper, thyme, and salt in a bowl. Rub mixture over all sides of the pork. Wrap and refrigerate at least 2 hours or overnight. Remove pork from the refrigerator 30 minutes before roasting.

2 Preheat oven to 425°F. Sprinkle the shallots in the bottom of a small roasting pan. Place pork on top and place the apples around sides. Sprinkle apples with sugar. Roast 25 minutes, until meat thermometer reaches 155°F. Transfer pork and apples to a serving platter and keep warm.

3 Stir the broth and wine into the roasting pan. Cook over high heat, stirring to loosen any browned bits, until reduced to ½ cup. Slice the pork and serve with apples and sauce. Makes 4 servings.

PER SERVING		DAILY GOAL
Calories	230	2,000 (F), 2,500 (M)
Total Fat	6 g	60 g or less (F), 70 g or less (M)
Saturated fat	2 g	20 g or less (F), 23 g or less (M)
Cholesterol	61 mg	300 mg or less
Sodium	473 mg	2,400 mg or less
Carbohydrates	25 g	250 g or more
Protein	20 g	55 g to 90 g

NOTES

LAMB CHOPS WITH MINTED VINEGAR SAUCE

Lamb and mint jelly is a classic combination and in this updated version we've used delicate loin chops, mellow balsamic vinegar, and garden fresh mint. Garlicky sautéed spinach and orzo pasta round out the menu.

▼ *Low-fat*
Prep time: 15 minutes
Cooking time: 13 to 16 minutes
○ *Degree of difficulty: easy*

 4 **tablespoons minced shallots**
 ½ **cup balsamic vinegar**
 2 **tablespoons chopped fresh mint**
 12 **small lamb loin chops (2½ ounces each), trimmed**
    Salt
    Freshly ground pepper
 1 **teaspoon olive oil**
 1 **tablespoon minced garlic**
 1 **large bunch spinach, washed and stems removed**

 8 **ounces orzo pasta, cooked according to package directions, drained**

1 Combine the shallots and vinegar in a small saucepan and cook over medium heat 3 minutes, until reduced and syrupy. Remove from heat and stir in the mint; set aside.

2 Dry the chops well with paper towels. Sprinkle both sides of chops with salt and pepper. Spray a large heavy skillet with vegetable cooking spray. Heat over medium-high heat. Brown chops 3 minutes per side for medium rare. Transfer to a warm serving platter. Strain vinegar-mint sauce and pour over chops. Cover and keep warm.

3 Heat the oil in a large skillet over high heat. Add the garlic and cook 30 seconds, until fragrant. Stir in the spinach and cook 1 to 2 minutes, until just wilted. Serve immediately with lamb chops and orzo. Makes 4 servings.

PER SERVING		DAILY GOAL
Calories	410	2,000 (F), 2,500 (M)
Total Fat	9 g	60 g or less (F), 70 g or less (M)
Saturated fat	3 g	20 g or less (F), 23 g or less (M)
Cholesterol	76 mg	300 mg or less
Sodium	117 mg	2,400 mg or less
Carbohydrates	47 g	250 g or more
Protein	33 g	55 g to 90 g

NOTES

LAMB KEBOBS WITH LEMON AND MINT

Whether you make these kebobs with lamb or beef, they're a great way to use the grill. Don't be stingy with the mint—use both dried and fresh for maximum flavor.

▼ *Low-fat*
▽ *Low-calorie*
  Prep time: 15 minutes plus marinating
  Grilling time: 5 to 15 minutes
○ *Degree of difficulty: easy*

¼ **cup fresh lemon juice**
2 **tablespoons vegetable oil**
2 **teaspoons minced garlic**
2 **teaspoons dried mint**
1 **teaspoon grated lemon peel**
1 **teaspoon salt**
⅛ **teaspoon freshly ground pepper**
1½ **pounds boneless, trimmed leg of lamb *or* beef sirloin, cut into 2-inch pieces**
1 **pound small zucchini, cut into 1 inch pieces**
8 **ounces fresh mushrooms**
1 **pint cherry tomatoes**
4 **green onions (white part only), cut into 1-inch pieces**
30 **fresh mint leaves**
3 **cups hot cooked rice**
1 **lemon, sliced, for garnish**

1 Combine the lemon juice, oil, garlic, mint, lemon peel, salt, and pepper in a small bowl.

2 Toss the lamb with 3 tablespoons of the marinade in a large, heavy-duty plastic storage bag. Combine the zucchini, mushrooms, tomatoes, and green onions in another storage bag. Add the remaining marinade, tossing to coat. Seal the bags and refrigerate 4 hours or overnight.

3 Remove meat from refrigerator 30 minutes before grilling. Prepare grill. Thread 6 skewers with meat and mint leaves. Thread 1 skewer each with zucchini, mushrooms, tomatoes, and green onions. Grill over medium-hot coals 12 to 15 minutes for lamb, 12 minutes for beef, 10 minutes for zucchini, 5 minutes for mushrooms, and 2 minutes each for green onions and tomatoes, turning each skewer frequently. Arrange the skewers of meat and vegetables on cooked rice and garnish with lemon wedges. Makes 6 servings.

PER SERVING		DAILY GOAL
Calories	360	2,000 (F), 2,500 (M)
Total Fat	10 g	60 g or less (F), 70 g or less (M)
Saturated fat	3 g	20 g or less (F), 23 g or less (M)
Cholesterol	76 mg	300 mg or less
Sodium	343 mg	2,400 mg or less
Carbohydrates	36 g	250 g or more
Protein	29 g	55 g to 90 g

NOTES

GRILLED CHICKEN CAESAR

We made this Caesar salad a main dish by tossing the trademark anchovy dressing with grilled chicken.

▼ *Low-fat*
▽ *Low-calorie*
   Prep time: 15 minutes
   Grilling time: 8 minutes
○ *Degree of difficulty: easy*

2 **cups fresh ½-inch bread cubes**
1 **clove garlic, minced**
2 **tablespoons fresh lemon juice**
2 **teaspoons anchovy paste**
½ **teaspoon salt**
¼ **teaspoon freshly ground pepper**
2 **tablespoons extra virgin olive oil**
1 **tablespoon finely chopped shallots**
4 **boneless, skinless chicken breast
   halves (1 pound)**
8 **cups torn romaine lettuce leaves
   Lemon wedges**

1 Preheat oven to 375°F. Toss the bread cubes with the garlic on a jelly-roll pan. Bake 10 minutes, until golden.

2 Prepare grill or preheat broiler and broiler pan. Whisk the lemon juice with the anchovy paste, salt, and pepper in a medium bowl. Whisk in the oil and shallots until blended. Set aside.

3 Place the chicken between 2 sheets of wax paper. Pound the chicken gently to ¼ inch thickness with rolling pin or mallet. Sprinkle both sides with salt and pepper. Grill over medium coals or broil 3 inches from heat source, 4 minutes per side until opaque in center. Let chicken stand 5 minutes.

4 Meanwhile, toss the romaine and bread cubes with the dressing. Arrange salad on 4 plates. Slice the chicken and arrange on top of the greens and serve with lemon wedges. Makes 4 servings.

PER SERVING		DAILY GOAL
Calories	290	2,000 (F), 2,500 (M)
Total Fat	10 g	60 g or less (F), 70 g or less (M)
Saturated fat	2 g	20 g or less (F), 23 g or less (M)
Cholesterol	84 mg	300 mg or less
Sodium	579 mg	2,400 mg or less
Carbohydrates	13 g	250 g or more
Protein	37 g	55 g to 90 g

CHICKEN WITH SHIITAKE MUSHROOMS AND LEMON

Here's a dish that takes full advantage of the robust taste and texture of shiitake mushrooms. Be sure to trim the stems of these mushrooms before cooking them because they are tough. Serve the chicken with quick-cooking couscous.

▼ *Low-fat*
▽ *Low-calorie*
   Prep time: 15 minutes
   Cooking time: 13 to 16 minutes
○ *Degree of difficulty: easy*

4 **boneless, skinless chicken breast
   halves (1 pound)**
   Salt
   Freshly ground pepper
2 **teaspoons cornstarch**
2 **teaspoons vegetable oil**
½ **cup chopped onion**
8 **ounces fresh shiitake mushrooms,
   sliced**

1 can (13¾ or 14½ ounces) low-sodium chicken broth, defatted (see tip, page 9)
2 tablespoons fresh lemon juice
½ teaspoon grated lemon peel
½ teaspoon tarragon

1 Sprinkle both sides of the chicken pieces with salt and pepper. Toss chicken pieces in a medium bowl with cornstarch to coat.

2 Heat the oil in a large nonstick skillet over medium-high heat. Add chicken and cook until golden, 4 to 5 minutes per side. Transfer the chicken to a serving plate and keep warm.

3 Add the onion to skillet and cook, stirring 4 minutes, until tender. Add the mushrooms. Cover and cook 2 minutes; uncover and cook 2 minutes more. Stir in the broth, lemon juice, lemon peel, and tarragon. Cook, uncovered, until reduced by half. Return chicken to skillet. Cook 1 to 2 minutes, until heated through, turning once. Makes 4 servings.

PER SERVING		DAILY GOAL
Calories	185	2,000 (F), 2,500 (M)
Total Fat	4 g	60 g or less (F), 70 g or less (M)
Saturated fat	1 g	20 g or less (F), 23 g or less (M)
Cholesterol	66 mg	300 mg or less
Sodium	360 mg	2,400 mg or less
Carbohydrates	7 g	250 g or more
Protein	29 g	55 g to 90 g

CHICKEN MARSALA

Marsala is Italy's most famous fortified wine, and is available both as sweet and dry varieties. Either variety has a deep, smoky flavor which is perfect in this sauce. Serve Chicken Marsala with a side of polenta and a sprinkling of freshly grated Parmesan cheese.

▼ *Low-fat*
▽ *Low-calorie*
   Prep time: 10 minutes
   Cooking time: 20 to 28 minutes
○ *Degree of difficulty: easy*

4 boneless, skinless chicken breast halves (1 pound)
½ teaspoon salt
¼ teaspoon freshly ground pepper
¼ teaspoon sage
1 teaspoon vegetable oil
½ cup finely chopped onion
8 ounces fresh mushrooms, sliced
¼ cup Marsala wine
½ cup chicken broth, defatted (see tip, page 9)
1 tablespoon minced fresh parsley

1 Sprinkle both sides of the chicken with the salt, pepper, and sage. Heat the oil in a large nonstick skillet over medium-high heat. Add chicken and cook 4 minutes per side, until golden. Transfer the chicken to a serving plate and keep warm.

2 Add the onion to skillet and cook, stirring, 3 to 5 minutes, until tender. Add the mushrooms and cook, stirring, 5 minutes more. Stir in the wine and broth. Bring to boil and cook about 5 minutes, until reduced by half. Pour the sauce over the chicken and sprinkle with parsley. Makes 4 servings.

PER SERVING		DAILY GOAL
Calories	185	2,000 (F), 2,500 (M)
Total Fat	3 g	60 g or less (F), 70 g or less (M)
Saturated fat	1 g	20 g or less (F), 23 g or less (M)
Cholesterol	66	300 mg or less
Sodium	497 mg	2,400 mg or less
Carbohydrates	6 g	250 g or more
Protein	28 g	55 g to 90 g

NOTES

_____

_____

_____

_____

BALSAMIC CHICKEN WITH ORZO

The rich, mellow flavor of balsamic vinegar is given just a touch of sweetness with the addition of sautéed shallots and brown sugar. Orzo pasta helps soak up all the luscious juices.

▼ *Low-fat*
Prep time: 10 minutes
Cooking time: 16 minutes
○ *Degree of difficulty: easy*

4 **boneless, skinless chicken breast halves (1 pound)**
½ **teaspoon salt**
¼ **teaspoon freshly ground pepper**
1 **tablespoon olive oil**
¼ **cup minced shallots**
½ **cup chicken broth, defatted (see tip, page 9)**
3 **tablespoons balsamic vinegar**
1 **teaspoon brown sugar**
1 **tablespoon butter *or* margarine**
1 **cup orzo pasta, cooked according to package directions, drained**
2 **tablespoons minced fresh parsley**

1 Place the chicken between 2 sheets of wax paper. Pound to ½ inch thickness with a rolling pin or mallet. Sprinkle chicken with salt and pepper.

2 Heat the oil in a large skillet over medium-high heat. Cook chicken 4 minutes per side, until opaque in center. Transfer the chicken to a serving plate, cover, and keep warm.

3 Add the shallots to skillet and cook, stirring, 2 minutes. Add the broth, vinegar, and brown sugar. Bring to boil; cook about 4 minutes, until reduced by a third. Whisk the butter into skillet until melted. Pour the sauce over chicken. Toss the orzo with parsley and serve with the chicken. Makes 4 servings.

PER SERVING		DAILY GOAL
Calories	385	2,000 (F), 2,500 (M)
Total Fat	9 g	60 g or less (F), 70 g or less (M)
Saturated fat	3 g	20 g or less (F), 23 g or less (M)
Cholesterol	74 mg	300 mg or less
Sodium	527 mg	2,400 mg or less
Carbohydrates	41 g	250 g or more
Protein	33 g	55 g to 90 g

1. Slim sauce: Toss cooked pasta with tomato-based sauces or stir-fried vegetables instead of creamy sauces.

2. Pass the bread: Buy a different whole-grain bread each time you go shopping. Try cracked wheat, oatmeal, or five-grain varieties for starters.

3. Less is best: When preparing packaged mixes of rice, pasta, or stuffing, use only half the butter or margarine called for in the directions—you'll lose fat, not flavor.

4. Fruit not fat: Top bread, toast, bagels, and muffins with nonfat fruit spread or jam instead of butter, margarine, or cream cheese.

5. Read the label: Compare package labels on crackers for fat grams because they vary greatly.

6. Nutritious noshing: When you get the munchies, snack on foods like air-popped popcorn, pretzels, baked pita or tortilla crisps, half a bagel or English muffin, a few crackers, or some breadsticks.

20 WAYS TO MAKE MEALS HEALTHIER

7. Good 'n' plenty: Buy a variety of grains. There are many quick-cooking types to choose from, including bulgur wheat, quinoa, and barley, any of which can be used as the base of a nutritious entrée or side dish.

8. Sweet dreams: Healthful dessert choices can include fruit sorbets, a whole-grain waffle topped with frozen yogurt, or rice pudding.

9. Pile it on: Heap veggies onto your favorite sandwich: Stuff a tuna pita with shredded carrots and red cabbage; layer grilled vegetables on a turkey sandwich; or top a burger with romaine lettuce, fresh tomato, and cucumber slices.

10. Made to order: If you think healthful eating requires more time-consuming food preparation, take another look at the salad-bar section of the supermarket. Ready-to-go veggies are easy to add to salads, stir-fries, soups, pasta toppings, and side dishes.

11. Beans, beans: Canned beans are just as nutritious as dry beans and peas. Just drain and rinse them well before adding to soup, chili, salad, tacos, or rice dishes.

12. Flash in the pan: Use plain, unsauced frozen vegetables as a healthful choice for hurry-up meals. Boil, steam, or microwave to toss into salads, rice pilaf, or couscous.

13. Grill crazy: The next time you barbeque, place a few bell peppers, onions, or zucchini halves onto the grill along with your beef, chicken, or fish.

14. Muffin madness: To get more nutrition from your morning muffin, buy or bake muffins enhanced with fruit or vegetables. Pumpkin, butternut squash, zucchini, carrot, or cranberry are all delicious ingredients. When buying muffins, keep in mind that oversize muffins will be higher in fat.

15. Ace in the whole: Eat whole fruits often; they provide more fiber than fruit juice, especially when unpeeled. Introduce your family to new fruits. Some delicious tropical fruits to sample: include mango, papaya, guava, starfruit, red bananas, and unusual varieties of apples, plums, and melons.

16. Road food: Keep a supply of dried fruits in the pantry for easy, totable snacking.

17. Ice 'n' easy: Freeze canned pears or peaches in heavy syrup, then purée them in a food processor for a quick sorbet.

18. Don't say cheese: Cut back to ¼ to ⅓ on shredded cheese in traditional recipes for enchiladas and macaroni and cheese, and use reduced-fat cheese.

19. Hidden assets: Sneak dairy into your kid's diets by preparing canned soups with skim or low-fat milk instead of water.

20. Project lean: Always read labels at the meat counter to avoid hidden fat. Look for ground turkey or chicken that contains breast meat only. Choose at least 90% lean (or extra-lean) ground beef for your burgers. There are even lean hot dogs available.

BUFFALO-STYLE CHICKEN BREASTS WITH GORGONZOLA DIPPING SAUCE

We've kept all the great flavor of the famous zesty chicken wings, but eliminated lots of the fat by using skinless breasts and plain, nonfat yogurt. If you love all the heat of the original, just serve the breasts with a bottle of hot pepper sauce.

▼ *Low-fat*
▽ *Low-calorie*
   Prep time: 10 minutes plus chilling
   Grilling time: 12 minutes
○ *Degree of difficulty: easy*

Gorgonzola Dipping Sauce
  1 **cup plain nonfat yogurt**
  1 **tablespoon crumbled Gorgonzola cheese**
  1 **teaspoon fresh lemon juice**

  2 **teaspoons vegetable oil**
  1 **teaspoon paprika**
  ¾ **teaspoon salt**
  ½ **teaspoon ground red pepper**
  ¼ **teaspoon freshly ground pepper**
  4 **boneless, skinless chicken breast halves (about 1½ pounds)**
  1 **bulb fennel (anise) *or* 6 stalks celery, cut into sticks**

1 For Gorgonzola Dipping Sauce, line a mesh sieve with a paper towel or coffee filter and place it over a bowl. Add the yogurt and refrigerate 2 hours. Discard any liquid that accumulates in the bowl; transfer ½ cup of the drained yogurt to a medium bowl (reserve any remaining yogurt for another use). Stir in the cheese and lemon juice.

2 Prepare grill and lightly oil grill rack. Combine the oil, paprika, salt, ground red pepper, and freshly ground pepper to form a paste in a medium bowl. Add the chicken and toss with paste mixture until well coated. Grill over medium-hot coals 6 minutes per side. Serve immediately with sliced fennel and the Gorgonzola Dipping Sauce. Makes 4 servings.

PER SERVING WITH 2 TABLESPOONS SAUCE		DAILY GOAL
Calories	250	2,000 (F), 2,500 (M)
Total Fat	5 g	60 g or less (F), 70 g or less (M)
Saturated fat	1 g	20 g or less (F), 23 g or less (M)
Cholesterol	100 mg	300 mg or less
Sodium	649 mg	2,400 mg or less
Carbohydrates	5 g	250 g or more
Protein	43 g	55 g to 90 g

NOTES

OLD-FASHIONED CHICKEN AND BISCUITS

You'll love the flavor of this homey casserole featuring a cornucopia of vegetables and a tender, low-fat buttermilk biscuit topping. You can also prepare this with boneless, skinless turkey breast.

▼ *Low-fat*
▽ *Low-calorie*
  Prep time: 30 minutes
  Cooking time: 12 to 15 minutes
○ *Degree of difficulty: easy*

1 **can (13¾ *or* 14½ ounces) chicken broth, defatted (see tip, page 9) plus enough water to equal 3 cups**
4 **boneless, skinless chicken breast halves (1 pound)**
1 **cup thickly sliced carrots**
2 **cups diced yellow squash, cut into 1-inch pieces**
1 **cup trimmed, halved green beans**
½ **cup chopped green onions**
3 **tablespoons cornstarch**

1 **cup skim milk, divided**
½ **teaspoon dillweed**
½ **teaspoon salt**
⅛ **teaspoon freshly ground pepper**
   Pinch thyme
1 **cup frozen peas**

Biscuits
1 **cup all-purpose flour**
1 **teaspoon baking powder**
¼ **teaspoon baking soda**
¼ **teaspoon salt**
2 **tablespoons vegetable shortening**
½ **cup buttermilk**

1 Bring the broth and water to boil in a large saucepan over medium heat. Add the chicken; cover and simmer 10 minutes. Transfer the chicken with a slotted spoon to a bowl. Add the carrots to saucepan and cook 7 minutes. Add the squash, green beans, and green onions; cook 2 minutes more. Transfer vegetables with a slotted spoon to the bowl with the chicken.

2 Reheat the broth in saucepan over medium-low heat 1 minute. Stir the cornstarch into ¼ cup of the milk until smooth. Whisk milk mixture into broth along with the remaining ¾ cup milk, dillweed, salt, pepper, and thyme; bring to boil. Reduce heat and simmer 2 minutes.

3 Cut chicken into bite-size pieces. Stir chicken, cooked vegetables, and peas into sauce and cook until heated through. Transfer to a warm, shallow 2-quart casserole.

4 For Biscuits, preheat oven to 425°F. Lightly coat a cookie sheet with vegetable cooking spray. Combine the flour, baking powder, baking soda, and salt in a large bowl. With a pastry blender or 2 knives, cut in the shortening until mixture resembles coarse crumbs. Stir in the buttermilk just until dough holds together. Drop by tablespoonfuls onto prepared cookie sheet. Bake 12 to 15 minutes, until golden. Makes 1 dozen.

5 Top chicken mixture with hot Biscuits and serve immediately. Makes 6 servings.

PER SERVING WITH 2 BISCUITS		DAILY GOAL
Calories	290	2,000 (F), 2,500 (M)
Total Fat	7 g	60 g or less (F), 70 g or less (M)
Saturated fat	2 g	20 g or less (F), 23 g or less (M)
Cholesterol	46 mg	300 mg or less
Sodium	848 mg	2,400 mg or less
Carbohydrates	32 g	250 g or more
Protein	24 g	55 g to 90 g

CHICKEN TERIYAKI

Chicken hits the express lane with this quick-and-easy classic. Time is not a problem when this bird is paired with rice and sliced cucumbers tossed with rice wine vinegar—everything's ready in 20 minutes.

▼ *Low-fat*
▽ *Low-calorie*
   Prep time: 5 minutes
   Cooking time: 10 to 12 minutes
○ *Degree of difficulty: easy*

½ **cup chicken broth, defatted (see tip, page 9)**
3 **tablespoons reduced-sodium soy sauce**
2 **tablespoons rice wine vinegar**
1 **tablespoon honey**
1 **tablespoon vegetable oil**
4 **boneless, skinless chicken breast halves (1 pound)**
¼ **teaspoon freshly ground pepper**
4 **green onions, thinly sliced on the diagonal**
1 **tablespoon minced fresh ginger**
1 **teaspoon minced garlic**

1 Combine the chicken broth, soy sauce, vinegar, and honey in a medium bowl. Set aside.

2 Heat the oil in a large nonstick skillet over medium-high heat. Sprinkle the chicken with pepper. Cook chicken 4 to 5 minutes per side, until cooked through. Transfer the chicken to a platter and keep warm.

3 Add the green onions, ginger, and garlic to skillet and cook 1 minute. Stir in the soy sauce mixture and cook 1 minute more. Pour the sauce over the chicken. Makes 4 servings.

PER SERVING		DAILY GOAL	
Calories	220	2,000 (F), 2,500 (M)
Total Fat	6 g	60 g or less (F), 70 g or less (M)
Saturated fat	1 g	20 g or less (F), 23 g or less (M)
Cholesterol	82 mg	300 mg or less
Sodium	691 mg	2,400 mg or less
Carbohydrates	8 g	250 g or more
Protein	34 g	55 g to 90 g

113

CHICKEN À L'ORANGE

Try these fast, low-fat side dishes to go with this nutritious chicken: five-minute brown rice and crisp snow peas microwaved on high (100% power) for two minutes.

▼ *Low-fat*
▽ *Low-calorie*
  Prep time: 20 minutes
  Cooking time: 10 minutes
○ *Degree of difficulty: easy*

1 **tablespoon vegetable oil**
4 **boneless, skinless chicken breast halves (about 1½ pounds)**
½ **teaspoon salt**
¼ **teaspoon freshly ground pepper**
¾ **cup chopped green onions, divided**
1 **teaspoon cornstarch**
⅓ **cup chicken broth, defatted (see tip, page 9)**
2 **navel oranges, peeled and sectioned, juice reserved**
1 **tablespoon orange-flavored liqueur**
  Pinch ground red pepper

1 Heat the oil in a large skillet over medium-high heat. Pat the chicken dry with paper towels. Sprinkle chicken with salt and freshly ground pepper. Add chicken to skillet and cook 4 to 5 minutes per side, just until firm to the touch. Transfer the chicken to a platter and keep warm.

2 Add ½ cup of the onions to the skillet and cook 3 minutes, until tender. Combine the cornstarch and broth in a small bowl and stir until blended. Add to skillet with the orange sections and their juice, liqueur, and ground red pepper. Cook the sauce 1 minute more, until thickened. Spoon over chicken. Garnish with the remaining ¼ cup green onions. Makes 4 servings.

PER SERVING		DAILY GOAL
Calories	275	2,000 (F), 2,500 (M)
Total Fat	6 g	60 g or less (F), 70 g or less (M)
Saturated fat	1 g	20 g or less (F), 23 g or less (M)
Cholesterol	99 mg	300 mg or less
Sodium	481 mg	2,400 mg or less
Carbohydrates	12 g	250 g or more
Protein	40 g	55 g to 90 g

NOTES

114

MU SHU TURKEY

We've lightened up this classic from the Orient with boneless, skinless turkey breast and lots of vegetables. Tortillas are a convenient substitute for spring roll wrappers.

▼ *Low-fat*
▽ *Low-calorie*
   Prep time: 35 minutes plus standing
   Cooking time: 10 minutes
○ *Degree of difficulty: easy*

  4 **tablespoons reduced-sodium soy sauce, divided**
  1 **tablespoon fresh lime juice**
  1 **teaspoon minced jalapeño chile**
12 **ounces boneless, skinless turkey breast, cut into ½-inch-thick strips**
  2 **teaspoons vegetable oil, divided**
  1 **teaspoon minced garlic**
  ½ **teaspoon grated fresh ginger**
  2 **carrots, peeled and julienned**
  2 **tablespoons water**
  2 **cups shredded green cabbage**
  1 **zucchini, julienned**
  1 **cup thinly sliced fresh shiitake *or* white mushrooms**
  ¼ **teaspoon salt**
  2 **cups fresh bean sprouts**
  6 **flour tortillas (6-inch)**
  6 **teaspoons hoisin sauce**
  1 **cup fresh cilantro sprigs**
  3 **green onions, julienned**
    Hoisin sauce

1   Combine 3 tablespoons of the soy sauce, lime juice, and jalapeño in a medium bowl. Stir in the turkey and marinate 30 minutes.

2   Heat 1 teaspoon of the oil in a large nonstick skillet over medium-high heat. Add the garlic and ginger and cook 30 seconds. Stir in the carrots and 2 tablespoons water; cover and cook 1 minute. Stir in the cabbage, zucchini, mushrooms, the remaining 1 tablespoon soy sauce and the salt. Cook, covered, 2 minutes, until vegetables are just tender. Transfer the vegetables to a plate.

3   Heat the remaining 1 teaspoon oil in the same skillet. Add the turkey and cook, stirring, about 2 minutes, until turkey turns white and liquid is slightly reduced. Stir in the bean sprouts and reserved vegetables; heat through.

4   Spread each tortilla with 1 teaspoon hoisin sauce. Spoon about ¾ cup filling along the center, then top with cilantro and green onions. Roll the tortillas up and serve with additional hoisin sauce. Makes 6 servings.

Note: For Vegetarian Mu Shu: Prepare as directed, except omit 3 tablespoons soy sauce, the lime juice, jalapeño, and turkey. Cook the vegetables and prepare the tortillas as directed.

PER SERVING		DAILY GOAL
Calories	195	2,000 (F), 2,500 (M)
Total Fat	4 g	60 g or less (F), 70 g or less (M)
Saturated fat	0 g	20 g or less (F), 23 g or less (M)
Cholesterol	35 mg	300 mg or less
Sodium	706 mg	2,400 mg or less
Carbohydrates	23 g	250 g or more
Protein	19 g	55 g to 90 g

NOTES

FETTUCCINE BOLOGNESE

We've trimmed the fat by using lean ground beef and turkey in this hearty meat sauce, but kept all the traditional slow-simmered flavor. Use half this recipe and freeze the rest for those hectic days when you're too tired to cook.

▼   *Low-fat*
▽   *Low-calorie*
    Prep time: 25 minutes
    Cooking time: 1½ hours
○   *Degree of difficulty: easy*

2   **teaspoons olive oil**
8   **ounces lean (90%) ground beef**
8   **ounces ground turkey *or* chicken**
2   **cups chopped onions**
4   **teaspoons minced garlic**
½   **teaspoon salt**
½   **teaspoon freshly ground pepper**
½   **teaspoon thyme**
1   **pound fresh mushrooms, chopped**
1   **cup chopped carrots**
½   **cup chopped celery**
1   **can (13¾ *or* 14½ ounces) low-sodium beef broth, defatted (see tip, page 9)**
2   **cans (35 ounces each) plum tomatoes, with their liquid**
⅓   **cup tomato paste**
¼   **cup chopped fresh parsley**
1   **pound fettuccine, cooked according to package directions**

1   Heat the oil in a large Dutch oven over medium-high heat. Add the beef, turkey, and onions cook 5 minutes, until meat is no longer pink. Stir in the garlic, salt, pepper, and thyme and cook 30 seconds. Stir in the mushrooms and cook, covered, 5 minutes. Add the carrots and celery and cook, covered, 2 minutes more.

2   Stir the broth into mixture in Dutch oven. Bring to a boil and cook, uncovered, 10 minutes, until broth is slightly reduced. Stir in the tomatoes and their liquid and tomato paste, breaking up tomatoes with a spoon; return to a boil. Reduce heat and simmer, uncovered, 1 hour. Stir in the parsley. Reserve half the sauce for the fettuccine. Cool remaining sauce completely. Cover and freeze up to 1 month.

3   Drain the fettuccine and return to the pot. Add 5½ cups Bolognese Sauce, tossing to coat. Makes 6 servings.

PER SERVING		DAILY GOAL
Calories	420	2,000 (F), 2,500 (M)
Total Fat	8 g	60 g or less (F), 70 g or less (M)
Saturated fat	2 g	20 g or less (F), 23 g or less (M)
Cholesterol	97 mg	300 mg or less
Sodium	565 mg	2,400 mg or less
Carbohydrates	68 g	250 g or more
Protein	21 g	55 g to 90 g

NOTES

SPICE

IT UP

Here's a hot ticket to more healthful eating! Ladies' Home Journal® has zipped up today's light dishes with an assortment of fresh chile peppers and fragrant spices. You'll be tastefully surprised! Savor fiery classics like Grilled Five-Spice Steak; Pork and Poblano Stew; and Jamaican Jerk Chicken with Pineapple Salsa. And remember, spice adds variety to life.

PENNE ARRABBIATA

This vibrant tomato sauce gets its kick from a generous dose of red pepper flakes. You can also serve it with linguine or spaghetti.

▼ *Low-fat*
  Prep time: 15 minutes
  Cooking time: 22 minutes
○ *Degree of difficulty: easy*

1 **tablespoon olive oil**
½ **cup finely chopped onion**
1 **tablespoon minced garlic**
1 **teaspoon red pepper flakes**
½ **teaspoon salt**
1 **can (28 ounces) whole tomatoes, chopped with their liquid**
1 **pound penne, cooked according to package directions, drained**
¼ **cup chopped fresh parsley**

1 Heat the oil in a large skillet over medium heat. Add the onion and cook 5 minutes, until softened. Stir in the garlic, red pepper flakes, and salt and cook 30 seconds. Carefully add the tomatoes and their liquid. Cook, stirring occasionally, 15 minutes.

2 Toss the tomato sauce with the pasta and parsley in a large serving bowl. Makes 4 servings.

PER SERVING		DAILY GOAL
Calories	505	2,000 (F), 2,500 (M)
Total fat	6 g	60 g or less (F), 70 g or less (M)
Saturated fat	1 g	20 g or less (F), 23 g or less (M)
Cholesterol	0 mg	300 mg or less
Sodium	607 mg	2,400 mg or less
Carbohydrates	96 g	250 g or more
Protein	17 g	55 g to 90 g

NOTES

CHUNKY TURKEY AND BEAN CHILI

If a big bowl o' red is one of your sinful pleasures, you'll love the gutsy flavor of this version.

▼ *Low-fat*
▽ *Low-calorie*
  Prep time: 15 minutes plus chilling
  Cooking time: 20 minutes
○ *Degree of difficulty: easy*

1   **pound boneless turkey breast,**
    cut into 1-inch cubes
1   **teaspoon vegetable oil, divided**
1   **cup minced onions**
1   **tablespoon minced garlic**
2   **teaspoons chili powder**
½   **teaspoon cumin**
⅛   **teaspoon cinnamon**
1   **can (14½ *or* 16 ounces) tomatoes,**
    chopped with their liquid
1   **can (13¾ *or* 14½ ounces) chicken**
    broth, defatted (see tip, page 9)
1   **can (15 ounces) pinto beans,**
    drained and rinsed
1   **can (15 ounces) red kidney beans,**
    drained and rinsed
1   **package (10 ounces) frozen**
    succotash

1   Pat the turkey dry on paper towels. Heat ½ teaspoon of the oil in a large pot over high heat. Add half the turkey pieces and brown on all sides. Transfer turkey with a slotted spoon to a plate. Repeat with the remaining ½ teaspoon oil and turkey.

2   Add the onions to the pot. Cook, covered, over medium heat 5 minutes, until tender. Stir in the garlic, chili powder, cumin, and cinnamon. Cook 30 seconds. Carefully add the tomatoes and their liquid and bring to a boil. Add the chicken broth, pinto beans, kidney beans, and succotash; bring to a boil. Reduce heat and simmer 10 minutes. Add turkey and simmer 5 minutes more. Makes 8 cups.

PER CUP		DAILY GOAL	
Calories	195	2,000 (F), 2,500 (M)	
Total Fat	3 g	60 g or less (F), 70 g or less (M)	
Saturated fat	0 g	20 g or less (F), 23 g or less (M)	
Cholesterol	33 mg	300 mg or less	
Sodium	551 mg	2,400 mg or less	
Carbohydrates	23 g	250 g or more	
Protein	21 g	55 g to 90 g	

121

SINGAPORE TURKEY

This dish from the Philippines is a wonderful blend of sweet and sour flavors and is garnished with pineapple and cilantro-flavored rice. *Also pictured on page 118.*

Ⓜ *Microwave*
▼ *Low-fat*
▽ *Low-calorie*
   Prep time: 10 minutes
   Cooking time: 13 to 15 minutes
Ⓞ *Degree of difficulty: easy*

1 **pound boneless, skinless turkey breast, cut into 1½-inch chunks**
1 **tablespoon cornstarch**
1½ **teaspoons vegetable oil**
1 **tablespoon minced garlic**
½ **cup chicken broth, defatted (see tip, page 9)**
⅓ **cup low-sodium soy sauce**
⅓ **cup white vinegar**
½ **bay leaf**
2 **teaspoons granulated sugar**
¼ **teaspoon freshly ground pepper**
4 **ounces snow peas, trimmed**

1 **cup diced fresh *or* canned pineapple**
1 **cup long-grain rice, cooked according to package directions**
¼ **cup chopped fresh cilantro**

1 Toss the turkey and cornstarch to coat in a medium bowl. Heat the oil in a large skillet over medium-high heat. Add turkey and cook until browned, 3 to 4 minutes. Stir in the garlic and cook 1 minute more.

2 Stir in the chicken broth, soy sauce, vinegar, bay leaf, sugar, and pepper; bring to a boil. Reduce heat, then cover and simmer, stirring occasionally, 5 to 6 minutes, until turkey is cooked through. With a slotted spoon, transfer the turkey to a platter and keep warm. Discard bay leaf. Increase heat to high and cook sauce 5 minutes, until syrupy.

3 Meanwhile, place the snow peas in a microwave-proof dish. Sprinkle with 1 tablespoon water; cover and microwave on high (100% power) for 50 seconds. Drain and toss with turkey on serving platter. Arrange the pineapple around turkey on platter and pour over sauce. Stir the cilantro into the rice and serve with turkey. Makes 4 servings.

PER SERVING		DAILY GOAL
Calories	380	2,000 (F), 2,500 (M)
Total Fat	3 g	60 g or less (F), 70 g or less (M)
Saturated fat	1 g	20 g or less (F), 23 g or less (M)
Cholesterol	70 mg	300 mg or less
Sodium	997 mg	2,400 mg or less
Carbohydrates	52 g	250 g or more
Protein	34 g	55 g to 90 g

NOTES

123

SOUTHWEST TURKEY KEBOBS

This will become a favorite recipe for warm weather entertaining. Large chunks of turkey breast are perfect for grilling, and because they're skinless, the flavor of the peppery marinade really comes through.

▼   *Low-fat*
    Prep time: 30 minutes plus marinating
    Grilling time: 20 minutes
○   *Degree of difficulty: easy*

2   **tablespoons fresh lemon juice**
    Salt
1   **teaspoon minced garlic**
½   **teaspoon red pepper flakes**
¼   **cup olive oil**
¼   **cup chopped fresh oregano** *or*
    1 teaspoon dried plus ¼ cup chopped fresh parsley
3   **pounds boneless, skinless turkey breast**
2   **large** *or* **3 small yellow peppers, cut into 1½-inch cubes**
4   **medium red onions, cut into 1½-inch cubes**
1½ **pounds zucchini, cut into ¾-inch slices**

1 Whisk the lemon juice, 1 teaspoon salt, garlic, and red pepper flakes in a large bowl. Gradually whisk in the oil until blended. Stir in the oregano.

2 Cut the turkey into 1½-inch chunks, discarding any tough membrane. Add the turkey to the marinade, tossing to coat. Cover and refrigerate at least 4 hours. (Can be made ahead. Cover and refrigerate up to 24 hours.)

3 Prepare grill. Thread turkey alternately with the vegetables on 8 skewers. Sprinkle with salt. Grill over medium-hot coals, turning occasionally, 20 minutes, until turkey is cooked through. Makes 8 servings.

PER SERVING		DAILY GOAL
Calories	275	2,000 (F), 2,500 (M)
Total Fat	5 g	60 g or less (F), 70 g or less (M)
Saturated fat	1 g	20 g or less (F), 23 g or less (M)
Cholesterol	106 mg	300 mg or less
Sodium	232 mg	2,400 mg or less
Carbohydrates	12 g	250 g or more
Protein	45 g	55 g to 90 g

NOTES

TURKEY CUTLETS WITH PEPPERS AND PINEAPPLE

Sweet and hot flavors mingle in this fragrant dish inspired by the cooking of Southeast Asia.

▼ *Low-fat*
▽ *Low-calorie*
  Prep time: 20 minutes plus chilling
  Cooking time: 9 to 10 minutes
○ *Degree of difficulty: easy*

2	tablespoons minced fresh ginger
1	tablespoon minced lemon grass *or* 1 teaspoon grated lemon peel
1	jalapeño chile, seeded and minced
1	clove garlic, minced
1	pound turkey cutlets, ½ inch thick
1	tablespoon olive oil
1	green onion, sliced diagonally
2½	cups shredded savoy cabbage
½	large red pepper, julienned
½	large yellow pepper, julienned
½	large green pepper, julienned
2	cups cubed fresh pineapple
½	cup chicken broth, defatted (see tip, page 9)
2	tablespoons low-sodium soy sauce

1 Combine the ginger, lemon grass, jalapeño, and garlic in a medium bowl. Add the turkey cutlets and toss to coat. Cover and refrigerate 1 to 2 hours.

2 Prepare grill or preheat broiler. Heat the oil in a 10-inch nonstick skillet over medium-high heat. Add the green onion and cook until lightly browned. Add the cabbage and cook until it begins to brown, about 1 minute. Add red, yellow, and green peppers and cook 2 minutes. Stir in the pineapple and chicken broth. Cook until heated through, 3 minutes more. Set aside and keep warm.

3 Grill or broil turkey 3 to 4 minutes, until cooked through, turning once. Transfer the turkey to a serving platter and drizzle with the soy sauce. Spoon pepper-pineapple mixture around turkey. Makes 4 servings.

PER SERVING		DAILY GOAL
Calories	155	2,000 (F), 2,500 (M)
Total Fat	3 g	60 g or less (F), 70 g or less (M)
Saturated fat	.5 g	20 g or less (F), 23 g or less (M)
Cholesterol	47 mg	300 mg or less
Sodium	484 mg	2,400 mg or less
Carbohydrates	11 g	250 g or more
Protein	20 g	55 g to 90 g

NOTES

THAI CHICKEN-COCONUT SOUP

Fish sauce, fresh ginger, and coconut milk are the foundation of Thai cooking. They make a very refreshing, exotic soup in less than thirty minutes.

▼ *Low-fat*
▽ *Low-calorie*
   Prep time: 15 minutes
   Cooking time: 10 minutes
○ *Degree of difficulty: easy*

4 **cups chicken broth, defatted (see tip, page 9)**
2 **tablespoons fresh lime juice**
1 **tablespoon fish sauce (nuoc mam)* *or* ½ teaspoon anchovy paste**
4 **thin slices fresh ginger**
1 **pound boneless, skinless chicken thighs, trimmed and cut into ¼-inch-thick strips**
½ **cup unsweetened coconut milk***
⅛ **teaspoon red pepper flakes**
8 **ounces snow peas, trimmed and halved if large**
1 **cup shredded carrots**
¼ **cup chopped fresh cilantro**
2 **cups cooked rice**

1 Bring the chicken broth, lime juice, fish sauce, and ginger to a boil in a large saucepan. Reduce heat and simmer 3 minutes.

2 Add the chicken strips, coconut milk, and red pepper flakes. Return to a boil and simmer 4 minutes, until chicken is cooked through.

3 Add the snow peas and carrots; cook 1 minute, until peas are tender-crisp. Stir in the cilantro. Serve in soup bowls with cooked rice. Makes 4 servings.

*Available in Asian markets and specialty sections of supermarkets.

PER SERVING		DAILY GOAL
Calories	405	2,000 (F), 2,500 (M)
Total Fat	13 g	60 g or less (F), 70 g or less (M)
Saturated fat	6 g	20 g or less (F), 23 g or less (M)
Cholesterol	94 mg	300 mg or less
Sodium	1,274 mg	2,400 mg or less
Carbohydrates	39 g	250 g or more
Protein	30 g	55 g to 90 g

FIRE IT UP WITH GREAT SALSAS, DIPS, AND TOPPERS

This assortment of dips and toppers is a sure fire way to add zest to any healthy main dish. They also make great appetizers paired with crudités, crunchy baked tortilla chips, or pita wedges.

CLASSIC SALSA CRUDA

▼ *Low-fat*
▽ *Low-calorie*
　Prep time: 10 minutes
○ *Degree of difficulty: easy*

Place ⅓ cup finely diced onion in a wire mesh sieve and rinse under cold water. Drain and pat dry on paper towels. Combine the onion; 1 large tomato, seeded and cut into ¼-inch dice; 1 tablespoon chopped fresh cilantro; 1 teaspoon olive oil; ½ teaspoon minced jalapeño or serrano chile; and ¼ teaspoon salt in a large bowl. Makes 2 cups.

PER 1/4 CUP		DAILY GOAL
Calories	10	2,000 (F), 2,500 (M)
Total Fat	1 g	60 g or less (F), 70 g or less (M)
Saturated fat	0 g	20 g or less (F), 23 g or less (M)
Cholesterol	0 mg	300 mg or less
Sodium	69 mg	2,400 mg or less
Carbohydrates	1 g	250 g or more
Protein	0 g	55 g to 90 g

SPICY BLACK BEAN SALSA

▼ *Low-fat*
▽ *Low-calorie*
　Prep time: 20 minutes
　Cooking time: 15 minutes
○ *Degree of difficulty: easy*

Heat 1 tablespoon of olive oil in a large skillet over medium-high heat. Add ½ cup chopped onion, ¼ cup shredded carrot, 2 teaspoons minced jalapeño chile, 1 teaspoon cumin, ½ teaspoon chili powder, and ¼ teaspoon each salt and freshly ground pepper. Cook, stirring, until the onion is translucent and tender, 2 to 3 minutes. Stir in 1 cup frozen or canned corn, rinsed and drained; 1 cup canned black beans, rinsed and drained; ½ cup diced plum tomatoes; and 2 tablespoons chopped fresh cilantro. Heat through. Makes 3½ cups.

PER 1/4 CUP		DAILY GOAL
Calories	35	2,000 (F), 2,500 (M)
Total Fat	1 g	60 g or less (F), 70 g or less (M)
Saturated fat	0 g	20 g or less (F), 23 g or less (M)
Cholesterol	0 mg	300 mg or less
Sodium	78 mg	2,400 mg or less
Carbohydrates	5 g	250 g or more
Protein	2 g	55 g to 90 g

LIGHT GUACAMOLE TOPPER

▼ *Low-fat*
▽ *Low-calorie*
  Prep time: 10 minutes
○ *Degree of difficulty: easy*

Mash 1 ripe avocado with 2 tablespoons fresh lime juice in a small bowl. Stir in ½ cup plain nonfat yogurt, 1 tablespoon minced red onion, ¼ teaspoon salt, ¼ teaspoon ground red pepper, and a pinch of cumin. Makes 1½ cups.

PER TABLESPOON		DAILY GOAL
Calories	15	2,000 (F), 2,500 (M)
Total Fat	1 g	60 g or less (F), 70 g or less (M)
Saturated fat	0 g	20 g or less (F), 23 g or less (M)
Cholesterol	0 mg	300 mg or less
Sodium	27 mg	2,400 mg or less
Carbohydrates	1 g	250 g or more
Protein	0 g	55 g to 90 g

HERBED YOGURT-CHEESE TOPPER

▼ *Low-fat*
▽ *Low-calorie*
  Prep time: 10 minutes plus standing
○ *Degree of difficulty: easy*

Line a mesh sieve with a paper towel or a coffee filter and place it over a bowl. Spoon in 16 ounces plain low-fat yogurt. Place the strainer over a bowl at least 1 inch above the bottom of bowl and refrigerate, covered, overnight. Scoop the thickened yogurt into a small bowl. Stir in ¼ teaspoon minced garlic, ¼ teaspoon thyme, and ⅛ teaspoon each salt and freshly ground pepper. Let stand 30 minutes for flavors to blend. Makes ¾ cup.

PER TABLESPOON		DAILY GOAL
Calories	20	2,000 (F), 2,500 (M)
Total Fat	.5 g	60 g or less (F), 70 g or less (M)
Saturated fat	0 g	20 g or less (F), 23 g or less (M)
Cholesterol	1 mg	300 mg or less
Sodium	35 mg	2,400 mg or less
Carbohydrates	1 g	250 g or more
Protein	2 g	55 g to 90 g

WHITE BEAN DIP

▼ *Low-fat*
▽ *Low-calorie*
  Prep time: 10 minutes
○ *Degree of difficulty: easy*

Combine 1 can (15½ ounces) cannellini beans, drained and rinsed; 1 tablespoon fresh lemon juice; 2 tablespoons plain nonfat yogurt; 1 tablespoon chopped fresh parsley; ¼ teaspoon red pepper sauce; and ¼ teaspoon each salt and freshly ground pepper in a food processor. Process until smooth. Transfer the dip to a small bowl and stir in 1 teaspoon minced garlic. Makes 1¼ cups.

PER TABLESPOON		DAILY GOAL
Calories	20	2,000 (F), 2,500 (M)
Total Fat	.1 g	60 g or less (F), 70 g or less (M)
Saturated fat	0 g	20 g or less (F), 23 g or less (M)
Cholesterol	0 mg	300 mg or less
Sodium	57 mg	2,400 mg or less
Carbohydrates	3 g	250 g or more
Protein	1 g	55 g to 90 g

CHICKEN SKEWERS WITH INDONESIAN KETCHUP

This recipe, adapted from "Big Flavors of the Hot Sun," by Chris Schlesinger and John Willoughby (Morrow 1994), is a version of satay, the grilled skewers of Southeast Asia. We turn up the heat with a soy-lime-chile marinade, complemented by a soy-molasses sauce.

▼ *Low-fat*
▽ *Low-calorie*
   Prep time: 45 minutes plus marinating
   Grilling time: 4 to 6 minutes
○ *Degree of difficulty: easy*

Indonesian Ketchup
½ **cup light molasses**
½ **cup reduced-sodium soy sauce**
½ **cup firmly packed brown sugar**
2 **tablespoons cracked black pepper**
2 **tablespoons minced fresh ginger**
1 **teaspoon nutmeg**

8 **boneless, skinless chicken breast halves (2 pounds)**
½ **cup water**
¼ **cup fresh lime juice**
¼ **cup reduced-sodium soy sauce**
2 **to 4 tablespoons minced jalapeño *or* serrano chiles**
1 **tablespoon cracked black pepper**

1 For Indonesian Ketchup, combine molasses, soy sauce, brown sugar, pepper, ginger, and nutmeg in a medium saucepan; bring to a boil. Reduce heat and simmer, stirring frequently, 7 to 10 minutes, until slightly thickened. (Can be made ahead. Cover and refrigerate up to 1 month.)

2 Cut the chicken breasts into 3x½-inch strips. Combine the water, lime juice, soy sauce, jalapeño chiles, and pepper in a medium glass bowl. Add the chicken and toss to coat. Cover and refrigerate 3 to 4 hours, stirring once or twice.

3 Prepare grill. Remove chicken from marinade and thread loosely on metal skewers. Grill over medium-hot coals 2 to 3 minutes per side, until cooked through and browned. Just before removing from grill,

brush lightly with Indonesian Ketchup. Serve with additional Indonesian Ketchup for dipping. Makes 8 servings.

PER SERVING		DAILY GOAL
Calories	255	2,000 (F), 2,500 (M)
Total Fat	2 g	60 g or less (F), 70 g or less (M)
Saturated fat	0 g	20 g or less (F), 23 g or less (M)
Cholesterol	66 mg	300 mg or less
Sodium	955 mg	2,400 mg or less
Carbohydrates	32 g	250 g or more
Protein	28 g	55 g to 90 g

NOTES

131

MADRAS CHICKEN AND VEGETABLES

Boneless, skinless chicken breasts can be used interchangeably with thighs in this recipe, but remember, thighs take a bit longer to cook. We've added just a touch of tomato paste to enhance the color and flavor of this curry sauce.

▼ *Low-fat*
▽ *Low-calorie*
  Prep time: 10 minutes
  Cooking time: 16 to 19 minutes
○ *Degree of difficulty: easy*

2 **tablespoons curry powder**
1 **teaspoon cumin**
¾ **teaspoon salt**
¼ **teaspoon freshly ground pepper**
  Pinch cloves
2 **tablespoons water**
1 **teaspoon minced garlic**
1 **teaspoon tomato paste**
1 **tablespoon vegetable oil**
2 **cups finely chopped onions**

8 **boneless, skinless chicken thighs**
  (1¼ pounds), halved
1 **Golden Delicious apple, cored and**
  cut into 1-inch pieces
1 **cup sliced (½-inch) carrots**
¾ **cup chicken broth, defatted**
  (see tip, page 9)
1 **cup frozen peas, thawed**
1 **cup couscous *or* long-grain rice,**
  cooked according to package
  directions

1 Combine the curry powder, cumin, salt, pepper, cloves, water, garlic, and tomato paste in a small bowl. Stir until blended and set aside.

2 Heat the oil in Dutch oven over high heat. Add the onions and cook, stirring occasionally, 3 to 4 minutes, until tender. Add the spice mixture and cook until fragrant, 1 minute. Add the chicken, apple, carrots, and broth. Reduce heat and simmer, covered, stirring occasionally, until chicken is cooked and apples are tender, 12 to 14 minutes. Stir in the peas and heat through. Serve with cooked couscous or rice. Makes 4 servings.

PER SERVING		DAILY GOAL
Calories	485	2,000 (F), 2,500 (M)
Total Fat	11 g	60 g or less (F), 70 g or less (M)
Saturated fat	2 g	20 g or less (F), 23 g or less (M)
Cholesterol	118 mg	300 mg or less
Sodium	814 mg	2,400 mg or less
Carbohydrates	61 g	250 g or more
Protein	35 g	55 g to 90 g

DOUBLE-ORANGE CHICKEN WITH GINGER

Fresh ginger and tangy orange juice and orange peel spice up this quick stir-fry. Serve it with whole wheat spaghetti.

▼ *Low-fat*
▽ *Low-calorie*
  Prep time: 20 minutes
○ *Cooking time: 12 minutes*
  Degree of difficulty: easy

⅓ **cup fresh orange juice**
¼ **cup reduced-sodium soy sauce**
1 **teaspoon cornstarch**
¼ **teaspoon grated orange peel**
  Pinch freshly ground pepper

- 12 ounces boneless, skinless chicken breast, sliced ½ inch thick
- ¼ cup water
- 3 cups chopped broccoli
- 2 teaspoons vegetable oil
- 1 teaspoon grated fresh ginger

1 Combine the orange juice, soy sauce, cornstarch, orange peel, and pepper in a medium bowl until smooth. Stir in the chicken and let stand 10 minutes.

2 Meanwhile, bring the water to a boil in a large nonstick skillet. Add the broccoli; cover and steam 3 minutes. Drain the broccoli and set aside. Wipe skillet dry.

3 Heat the oil in same skillet over medium-high heat. Add the ginger and cook 30 seconds, until fragrant. Add the chicken and marinade and cook, stirring, 4 to 5 minutes, until cooked through. Stir in the broccoli. Makes 4 servings.

PER SERVING		DAILY GOAL
Calories	155	2,000 (F), 2,500 (M)
Total Fat	4 g	60 g or less (F), 70 g or less (M)
Saturated fat	1 g	20 g or less (F), 23 g or less (M)
Cholesterol	49 mg	300 mg or less
Sodium	673 mg	2,400 mg or less
Carbohydrates	8 g	250 g or more
Protein	23 g	55 g to 90 g

CHICKEN POCKETS WITH HOISIN SAUCE

East meets West in this eclectic combination of tastes and textures wrapped up in a soft flour tortilla.

▼ *Low-fat*
▽ *Low-calorie*
Prep time: 20 minutes plus marinating
Cooking time: 8 minutes
○ *Degree of difficulty: easy*

- 2 tablespoons soy sauce
- 4 tablespoons balsamic vinegar, divided
- 1 teaspoon grated fresh ginger
- 1 teaspoon minced garlic
- ¼ teaspoon freshly ground pepper
- 4 boneless, skinless chicken breast halves (about 1 pound)
- 2 tablespoons hoisin sauce
- 8 flour tortillas (6-inch)
- 2 cups julienned jicama
- 2 cups julienned carrots
- 8 green onions, julienned

1 Combine the soy sauce, 2 tablespoons of the vinegar, ginger, garlic, and pepper in a medium bowl. Add the chicken breasts and toss to coat. Cover and refrigerate 1 hour.

2 Preheat broiler. Combine the hoisin sauce and the remaining 2 tablespoons vinegar in cup. Broil chicken 3 inches from heat source for 3 to 4 minutes per side, until opaque in center. On a cutting board, slice each breast lengthwise into ½-inch-thick strips.

3 For each pocket, spread 1 side of a tortilla with 1 teaspoon of the hoisin mixture. Place half of one sliced chicken breast in the center and top it with ¼ cup each jicama, carrot, and green onion, then roll the tortilla up over the filling. Repeat with remaining ingredients to make 7 more rolls. Makes 4 servings.

PER SERVING		DAILY GOAL
Calories	330	2,000 (F), 2,500 (M)
Total Fat	5 g	60 g or less (F), 70 g or less (M)
Saturated fat	1 g	20 g or less (F), 23 g or less (M)
Cholesterol	66 mg	300 mg or less
Sodium	1,062 mg	2,400 mg or less
Carbohydrates	39 g	250 g or more
Protein	33 g	55 g to 90 g

JAMAICAN JERK CHICKEN WITH PINEAPPLE SALSA

The heat is on! For Caribbean flavor in a flash, keep a jar of Jamaican jerk sauce on hand to jazz up your chicken. Convenient, precut fresh pineapple lets you whip up the salsa in seconds. *Also pictured on the cover.*

▼ *Low-fat*
▽ *Low-calorie*
  Prep time: 15 minutes
  Cooking time: 12 minutes
○ *Degree of difficulty: easy*

  1 **cup quick-cooking couscous**
  1 **tablespoon vegetable oil**
  4 **boneless, skinless chicken breast halves (1 pound)**
     Salt
     Freshly ground pepper
 ½ **cup chicken broth, defatted (see tip, page 9)**
  2 **tablespoons Jamaican jerk sauce***
  3 **green onions, sliced**

Pineapple Salsa
  1 **package (8 ounces) fresh, peeled and diced pineapple**
  1 **red pepper, diced**
 ½ **cup mango chutney**
 ¼ **cup chopped fresh cilantro**
     Lime wedges

1 Cook the couscous according to package directions.

2 Meanwhile, heat the oil in a large skillet over medium-high heat. Sprinkle both sides of the chicken with salt and pepper. Add the chicken to skillet and cook 4 to 5 minutes per side, until firm. Transfer the cooked chicken to serving plate and keep warm.

3 Add the chicken broth and jerk sauce to the skillet and bring to a boil; boil 1 minute. Pour the sauce over chicken and sprinkle with the green onions.

4 For Pineapple Salsa, combine the pineapple, red peppers, chutney, and cilantro in a medium bowl, stirring to combine.

5 Serve the chicken with the couscous, Pineapple Salsa, and lime wedges. Makes 4 servings.

*Jamaican jerk sauce is available in gourmet markets and the specialty section of some supermarkets.

PER SERVING		DAILY GOAL	
Calories	480	2,000 (F), 2,500 (M)	
Total Fat	6 g	60 g or less (F), 70 g or less (M)	
Saturated fat	1 g	20 g or less (F), 23 g or less (M)	
Cholesterol	68 mg	300 mg or less	
Sodium	646 mg	2,400 mg or less	
Carbohydrates	70 g	250 g or more	
Protein	34 g	55 g to 90 g	

NOTES

PORK AND POBLANO STEW

This stew boasts a double dose of fresh chile flavor from roasted poblanos and minced jalapeños. If it's a milder flavor you seek, substitute sweet green peppers for the poblanos.

▼ *Low-fat*
▽ *Low-calorie*
  Prep time: 35 minutes
  Cooking time: 2 hours 25 minutes
○ *Degree of difficulty: easy*

  4 poblano chiles *or* 2 green peppers
  1 tablespoon minced garlic
  1½ teaspoons salt, divided
  1½ pounds trimmed, lean boneless pork shoulder, cut into 1½-inch cubes
  3 cups finely chopped onions
  ¼ cup minced jalapeño chiles
  ½ teaspoon oregano
  1½ pounds red new potatoes, quartered
  ½ cup chopped fresh cilantro
  3 zucchini, halved lengthwise and sliced ½ inch thick

  1 package (10 ounces) frozen whole-kernel corn, thawed
     Lime wedges, for garnish

1 Preheat broiler. Roast the poblanos 5 inches from heat 25 minutes, turning every 5 minutes, until skin is charred. Cover and cool. As soon as cool enough to handle, peel the skin from the chiles with a small sharp knife; discard seeds and coarsely chop.

2 Preheat oven to 325°F. With the flat side of a large knife, crush the garlic with 1 teaspoon of the salt to form a paste. Combine the garlic paste with poblanos, pork, onions, jalapeños, and oregano in a large heavy Dutch oven. Cover and roast 1½ hours.

3 Stir in the potatoes and cilantro. Cover and cook 30 minutes. Add the zucchini, corn, and ½ teaspoon salt and cook 20 minutes more, until pork and vegetables are tender. Garnish with limes, if desired. Makes 10 cups.

PER CUP		DAILY GOAL
Calories	225	2,000 (F), 2,500 (M)
Total Fat	6 g	60 g or less (F), 70 g or less (M)
Saturated fat	2 g	20 g or less (F), 23 g or less (M)
Cholesterol	46 mg	300 mg or less
Sodium	394 mg	2,400 mg or less
Carbohydrates	28 g	250 g or more
Protein	17 g	55 g to 90 g

TANDOORI CHICKEN

The spicy yogurt marinade in this classic chicken dish from India tenderizes the meat, leaving it moist and succulent after broiling. Serve the chicken with nutty bulgur pilaf studded with currants and chopped parsley.

▼ *Low-fat*
▽ *Low-calorie*
  Prep time: 10 minutes plus standing
  Cooking time: 13 to 14 minutes
○ *Degree of difficulty: easy*

  1 teaspoon cumin
  1 teaspoon paprika
  ½ teaspoon coriander
  ½ teaspoon ground red pepper
  ¾ cup plain nonfat yogurt
  2 tablespoons fresh lemon juice
  1 tablespoon minced fresh ginger
  1 teaspoon minced garlic
  1 teaspoon salt
  4 boneless, skinless chicken breast halves (1 pound)

¼ **cup cilantro leaves, for garnish (optional)**
Lemon wedges, for garnish (optional)

1 Combine cumin, paprika, coriander, and red pepper in a small saucepan. Cook, stirring, over low heat until fragrant, 1 to 2 minutes. *(Be careful not to scorch.)* Transfer the spices to a medium bowl. Stir in the yogurt, lemon juice, ginger, garlic, and salt. Add the chicken, tossing to coat. Let stand 30 minutes or cover and refrigerate overnight.

2 Preheat broiler and foil-lined broiler pan. Remove chicken from marinade and broil 3 inches from heat 5 minutes. Turn and broil 7 minutes more or until chicken begins to brown. To serve, slice the chicken diagonally against the grain. Garnish with cilantro and lemon, if desired. Makes 4 servings.

PER SERVING		DAILY GOAL
Calories	160	2,000 (F), 2,500 (M)
Total Fat	2 g	60 g or less (F), 70 g or less (M)
Saturated fat	0 g	20 g or less (F), 23 g or less (M)
Cholesterol	67 mg	300 mg or less
Sodium	658 mg	2,400 mg or less
Carbohydrates	5 g	250 g or more
Protein	29 g	55 g to 90 g

NEGAMAKI

These tender beef rolls from the Far East are filled with green onions, quickly seared in a hot skillet, then plunged in a fragrant dipping sauce.

▼ *Low-fat*
▽ *Low-calorie*
  Prep time: 25 minutes
  Cooking time: 3 minutes
○ *Degree of difficulty: easy*

¼ **cup low-sodium soy sauce**
2 **tablespoons rice wine vinegar**
2 **tablespoons minced green onions**
1 **teaspoon grated fresh ginger**
½ **teaspoon Asian sesame oil**
⅛ **teaspoon granulated sugar**
4 **ounces green onion tops, cut into 2-inch pieces (about 1½ cups)**
1 **pound beef flank steak, cut across the grain into twenty 5-inch-long strips about ¼-inch thick**
Salt
Freshly ground pepper
1 **cup short-grain rice, cooked according to package directions**

1 Combine soy sauce, vinegar, green onions, ginger, sesame oil, and sugar in a small bowl.

2 Bring a small saucepan of water to a boil. Add the green onions and cook 20 seconds. Immediately drain and add to a bowl of cold water. Drain again and pat dry on paper towels.

3 Sprinkle both sides of beef strips with salt and pepper. Place 2 to 3 green onions at one end of each steak strip, then roll the meat up and secure with wooden toothpicks. Pat dry on paper towels.

4 Spray a large heavy skillet with vegetable cooking spray and heat over medium-high heat. Brown the beef rolls, turning frequently, 3 minutes for rare in the centers. Remove toothpicks and serve immediately with dipping sauce and rice. Makes 4 servings.

PER SERVING		DAILY GOAL
Calories	410	2,000 (F), 2,500 (M)
Total Fat	13 g	60 g or less (F), 70 g or less (M)
Saturated fat	5 g	20 g or less (F), 23 g or less (M)
Cholesterol	59 mg	300 mg or less
Sodium	684 mg	2,400 mg or less
Carbohydrates	43 g	250 g or more
Protein	27 g	55 g to 90 g

GRILLED FIVE-SPICE STEAK

A wonderful way to store extra fresh ginger is to peel and grate it, then cover it with dry sherry and refrigerate. Simply drain the desired amount of ginger before using it in your next recipe.

▽ *Low-calorie*
   Prep time: 20 minutes plus marinating
   Grilling time: 32 to 40 minutes
○ *Degree of difficulty: easy*

¼ **cup soy sauce**
1 **tablespoon minced fresh ginger**
1 **tablespoon minced garlic**
1½ **teaspoons vegetable oil**
1½ **teaspoons cider vinegar**
1 **teaspoon red pepper flakes**
1 **teaspoon five-spice powder***
1 **pound beef top round steak** *or*
   **1½ pounds center-cut leg of
   lamb steaks**
8 **ounces zucchini, cut lengthwise
   into ½-inch strips**
8 **ounces yellow squash, cut
   lengthwise into ½-inch strips**
1 **cup cherry tomato halves**
1 **bunch green onions, trimmed**

1 Combine the soy sauce, ginger, garlic, oil, vinegar, pepper flakes, and five-spice powder in a shallow dish. Add the meat to the marinade, turning to coat. Cover and refrigerate overnight.

2 One hour before grilling, remove meat from refrigerator. Prepare grill. Remove meat from marinade. Grill meat over medium coals 12 to 15 minutes per side for medium-rare. Let stand 10 minutes.

3 Meanwhile, arrange the zucchini, squash, tomatoes, and green onions on grill. Grill until vegetables are tender; 8 minutes for zucchini and squash, 5 minutes for green onions, and 2 minutes for tomatoes, turning once.

4 Slice meat very thinly across the grain and arrange it on a large platter with grilled vegetables. Makes 4 servings.

*Five-spice powder is available in the spice section at the supermarket and in Asian food markets.

PER SERVING		DAILY GOAL
Calories	330	2,000 (F), 2,500 (M)
Total Fat	13 g	60 g or less (F), 70 g or less (M)
Saturated fat	4 g	20 g or less (F), 23 g or less (M)
Cholesterol	104 mg	300 mg or less
Sodium	1,113 mg	2,400 mg or less
Carbohydrates	10 g	250 g or more
Protein	40 g	55 g to 90 g

NOTES

MANDARIN BEEF SALAD

Steak is great, but for a healthy diet it's important not to overindulge. Here's the perfect way to stretch the meat: Just broil your favorite flank steak one night and use the leftovers in this zesty salad with warm orange dressing the next.

▼ *Low-fat*
▽ *Low-calorie*
  Prep time: 15 minutes plus standing
  Cooking time: 5 minutes
○ *Degree of difficulty: easy*

⅓ **cup orange juice**
2 **tablespoons rice wine vinegar**
1 **teaspoon Asian sesame oil**
½ **teaspoon grated fresh ginger**
½ **teaspoon dry mustard**
½ **teaspoon salt**
⅛ **teaspoon red pepper flakes**
4 **cups torn romaine lettuce leaves**
2 **cups arugula**
1 **cup bean sprouts**
⅓ **cup julienned radishes**
8 **ounces thinly sliced broiled beef flank steak**

1 Combine the orange juice, vinegar, sesame oil, ginger, mustard, salt, and pepper flakes in a small saucepan. Let stand 1 hour.

2 Combine the romaine, arugula, bean sprouts, radishes, and flank steak in a large salad bowl. Heat the orange dressing over medium-low heat until warm and drizzle it over the salad, tossing well. Makes 4 servings.

PER SERVING		DAILY GOAL
Calories	170	2,000 (F), 2,500 (M)
Total Fat	8 g	60 g or less (F), 70 g or less (M)
Saturated fat	3 g	20 g or less (F), 23 g or less (M)
Cholesterol	38 mg	300 mg or less
Sodium	336 mg	2,400 mg or less
Carbohydrates	6 g	250 g or more
Protein	17 g	55 g to 90 g

NOTES

141

METRIC COOKING HINTS

By making a few conversions, cooks in Australia, Canada, and the United Kingdom can use the recipes in Ladies' Home Journal® *100 Great Healthy Main Dishes* with confidence. The charts on this page provide a guide for converting measurements from the U.S. customary system, which is used throughout this book, to the imperial and metric systems. There also is a conversion table for oven temperatures to accommodate the differences in oven calibrations.

Volume and Weight: Americans traditionally use cup measures for liquid and solid ingredients. The chart (top right) shows the approximate imperial and metric equivalents. If you are accustomed to weighing solid ingredients, here are some helpful approximate equivalents.
■ 1 cup butter, castor sugar, or rice = 8 ounces = about 250 grams
■ 1 cup flour = 4 ounces = about 125 grams
■ 1 cup icing sugar = 5 ounces = about 150 grams
  Spoon measures are used for smaller amounts of ingredients. Although the size of the tablespoon varies slightly among countries, for practical purposes and for recipes in this book, a straight substitution is all that's necessary.
  Measurements made using cups or spoons should always be level, unless stated otherwise.

Product Differences: Most of the ingredients called for in the recipes in this book are available in English-speaking countries. However, some are known by different names. Here are some common American ingredients and their possible counterparts:
■ Sugar is granulated or castor sugar.
■ Powdered sugar is icing sugar.
■ All-purpose flour is plain household flour or white flour. When self-rising flour is used in place of all-purpose flour in a recipe that calls for leavening, omit the leavening agent (baking soda or baking powder) and salt.
■ Light corn syrup is golden syrup.
■ Cornstarch is cornflour.
■ Baking soda is bicarbonate of soda.
■ Vanilla is vanilla essence.

USEFUL EQUIVALENTS

⅛ teaspoon = 0.5 ml	⅔ cup = 5 fluid ounces = 150 ml
¼ teaspoon = 1 ml	¾ cup = 6 fluid ounces = 175 ml
½ teaspoon = 2 ml	1 cup = 8 fluid ounces = 250 ml
1 teaspoon = 5 ml	2 cups = 1 pint
¼ cup = 2 fluid ounces = 50 ml	2 pints = 1 litre
⅓ cup = 3 fluid ounces = 75 ml	½ inch =1 centimetre
½ cup = 4 fluid ounces = 125 ml	1 inch = 2 centimetres

BAKING PAN SIZES

American	Metric
8x1½-inch round baking pan	20x4-centimetre sandwich or cake tin
9x1½-inch round baking pan	23x3.5-centimetre sandwich or cake tin
11x7x1½-inch baking pan	28x18x4-centimetre baking pan
13x9x2-inch baking pan	32.5x23x5-centimetre baking pan
2-quart rectangular baking dish	30x19x5-centimetre baking pan
15x10x2-inch baking pan	38x25.5x2.5-centimetre baking pan (Swiss roll tin)
9-inch pie plate	22x4- or 23x4-centimetre pie plate
7- or 8-inch springform pan	18- or 20-centimetre springform or loose-bottom cake tin
9x5x3-inch loaf pan	23x13x6-centimetre or 2-pound narrow loaf pan or paté tin
1½-quart casserole	1.5-litre casserole
2-quart casserole	2-litre casserole

OVEN TEMPERATURE EQUIVALENTS

Fahrenheit Setting	Celsius Setting*	Gas Setting
300°F	150°C	Gas Mark 2
325°F	160°C	Gas Mark 3
350°F	180°C	Gas Mark 4
375°F	190°C	Gas Mark 5
400°F	200°C	Gas Mark 6
425°F	220°C	Gas Mark 7
450°F	230°C	Gas Mark 8
Broil		Grill

Electric and gas ovens may be calibrated using Celsius. However, increase the Celsius setting 10 to 20 degrees when cooking above 160°C with an electric oven. For convection or forced-air ovens (gas or electric), lower the temperature setting 10°C when cooking at all heat levels.